NEW DIRECTIONS 23

N D

New Directions in Prose and Poetry 23

Edited by J. Laughlin

 A New Directions Book

ACKNOWLEDGMENTS

Grateful acknowledgment is made to the editors and publishers of books
and magazines where some of the selections in this book first appeared:
for Robert Bly, *Choice, Guabi, The Massachusetts Review, Tennessee
Poetry* and *Westigan Review;* for Besmilr Brigham, ARX Foundation,
Harper's Bazaar and Summit Press; for Robert Duncan, The Phoenix
Bookshop (Copyright © 1969 by Robert Duncan); for Lawrence Fer-
linghetti, *Notes from Underground;* for Walter S. Hamady, The Perish-
able Press (Copyright © 1969 by Walter S. Hamady); for Lawson
Fusao Inada, *December* and *Quixote;* for Richard Meyers, *Genesis: Grasp*
(Copyright © 1970 by *Genesis: Grasp*); for James Purdy, The Black
Sparrow Press (Copyright © 1970 by James Purdy); for Carl Rakosi,
The Iowa Review and *The Park;* for Gary Snyder, *The Center Magazine.*

Manufactured in the United States of America
First published clothbound and as New Directions Paperbook 315 in 1971
Published simultaneously in Canada by McClelland & Stewart, Ltd.

New Directions Books are published for James Laughlin
by New Directions Publishing Corporation,
333 Sixth Avenue, New York 10014

CONTENTS

THE WILDERNESS*

GARY SNYDER

I am a poet. My teachers are other poets, American Indians, and a
few Buddhist priests in Japan. The reason I am here is because I
wish to bring a voice from the wilderness, my constituency. I wish
to be a spokesman for a realm that is not usually represented either
in intellectual chambers or in the chambers of government.

I was climbing Glacier Peak in the Cascades of Washington several years ago, on one of the clearest days I had ever seen. When
we reached the summit of Glacier Peak we could see almost to the
Selkirks in Canada. We could see south far beyond the Columbia
River to Mount Hood and Mount Jefferson. And, of course, we
could see Mount Adams and Mount Rainier. We could see across
Puget Sound to the ranges of the Olympic Mountains. My companion, who is not a poet, said: "You mean, there is a senator for all
this?"

Unfortunately, there isn't a senator for all that. And I would like
to think of a new definition of humanism and a new definition of
democracy that would include the nonhuman, that would have
representation from those spheres. This is what I think we mean by
an ecological conscience.

I don't like Western culture because I think it has much in it that
is inherently wrong and that is at the root of the environmental

*Transcript of a statement made at a seminar at The Center for the
Study of Democratic Institutions, Santa Barbara, California.

crisis that is not recent; it is very ancient; it has been building up for a millennium. There are many things in Western culture that are admirable. But a culture that alienates itself from the very ground of its own being—from the wilderness outside (that is to say, wild nature, the wild, self-contained, self-informing eco-systems) and from that other wilderness, the wilderness within— is doomed to a very destructive behavior, ultimately perhaps self-destructive behavior.

The West is not the only culture that carries these destructive seeds. China had effectively deforested itself by 1000 A.D. India had effectively deforested itself by 800 A.D. The soils of the Middle East were ruined even earlier. The forests that once covered the mountains of Yugoslavia were stripped to build the Roman fleet, and those mountains have looked like Utah ever since. The soils of southern Italy and Sicily were ruined by latifundia slave-labor farming in the Roman Empire. The soils of the Atlantic seaboard in the United States were effectively ruined before the American Revolution because of the one-crop (tobacco) farming. So the same forces have been at work in East and West.

You would not think a poet would get involved in these things. But the voice that speaks to me as a poet, what Westerners have called the Muse, is the voice of nature herself, whom the ancient poets called the great goddess, the Magna Mater. I regard that voice as a very real entity. At the root of the problem where our civilization goes wrong is the mistaken belief that nature is some-thing less than authentic, that nature is not as alive as man is, or as intelligent, that in a sense it is dead, and that animals are of so low an order of intelligence and feeling, we need not take their feelings into account.

A line is drawn between primitive peoples and civilized peoples. I think there is a wisdom in the worldview of primitive peoples that we have to refer ourselves to, and learn from. If we are on the verge of postcivilization, then our next step must take account of the primitive worldview which has traditionally and intelligently tried to open and keep open lines of communication with the forces of nature. You cannot communicate with the forces of nature in the laboratory. One of the problems is that we simply do not know much about primitive people and primitive cultures. If we can tenta-tively accommodate the possibility that nature has a degree of authenticity and intelligence that requires that we look at it more sensitively, then we can move to the next step. "Intelligence" is not really the right word. The ecologist Eugene Odum uses the term "biomass."

Life-biomass, he says, is stored information; living matter is stored information in the cells and in the genes. He believes there is more information of a higher order of sophistication and complexity stored in a few square yards of forest than there is in all the libraries of mankind. Obviously, that is a different order of information. It is the information of the universe we live in. It is the information that has been flowing for millions of years. In this total information context, man may not be necessarily the highest or most interesting product.

Perhaps one of its most interesting experiments at the point of evolution, if we can talk about evolution in this way, is not man but a high degree of biological diversity and sophistication opening to more and more possibilities. Plants are at the bottom of the food chain; they do the primary energy transformation that makes all the life-forms possible. So perhaps plant life is what the ancients meant by the great goddess. Since plants support the other life-forms, they became the "people" of the land. And the land—a country—is a region within which the interactions of water, air, and soil and the underlying geology and the overlying (maybe stratospheric) wind conditions all go to create both the micro-climates and the large climactic patterns that make a whole sphere or realm of life possible. The people in that realm include animals, humans, and a variety of wild life.

What we must find a way to do, then, is incorporate the other people—what the Sioux Indians called the creeping people, and the standing people, and the flying people, and the swimming people—into the councils of government. This isn't as difficult as you might think. If we don't do it, they will revolt against us. They will submit nonnegotiable demands about our stay on the earth. We are beginning to get nonnegotiable demands right now from the air, the water, the soil.

I would like to expand on what I mean by representation here at the Center from these other fields, these other societies, these other communities. Ecologists talk about the ecology of oak communities, or pine communities. They *are* communities. This institute—this Center—is of the order of a kiva of elders. Its function is to maintain and transmit the lore of the tribe on the highest levels. If it were doing its job completely, it would have a cycle of ceremonies geared to the seasons, geared perhaps to the migrations of the fish and to the phases of the moon. It would be able to instruct in what rituals you follow when a child is born, when someone reaches puberty, when someone gets married, when someone dies. But, as you know, in these fragmented times, one council cannot perform all these functions at one time. Still it would be understood that a council of elders, the caretakers of the lore of the culture, would open themselves to representation from other life-forms. Historically this has been done through art. The paintings of bison and bears in the caves of southern France were of that order. The animals were speaking through the people and making their point. And when, in the dances of the Pueblo Indians and other peoples, certain individuals became seized, as it were, by the spirit of the deer, and danced as a deer would dance, or danced the dance of the corn maidens, or impersonated the squash blossom, they were no longer speaking for humanity, they were taking it on themselves to interpret, through their humanity, what these other life-forms were. That is about all we know so far concerning the possibilities of incorporating spokesmanship for the rest of life in our demo-cratic society.

Let me describe how a friend of mine from the Santo Domingo Pueblo hunts. He is twenty-seven years old. The Pueblo Indians, and I think probably most of the other Indians of the Southwest, begin their hunt, first, by purifying themselves. They take emetics, a sweat bath, and perhaps avoid their wife for a few days. They also try not to think certain thoughts. They go out hunting in an attitude of humility. They make sure that they need to hunt, that they are not hunting without necessity. Then they improvise a song while they are in the mountains. They sing aloud or hum to them-selves while they are walking along. It is a song to the deer, asking the deer to be willing to die for them. They usually still-hunt, taking a place alongside a trail. The feeling is that you are not hunting the deer, the deer is coming to you; you make yourself available for the deer that will present itself to you, that has given itself to you. Then you shoot it. After you shoot it, you cut the head off and place the head facing east. You sprinkle corn meal in front of the mouth of the deer, and you pray to the deer, asking it to forgive you for having killed it, to understand that we all need to eat, and to please make a good report to the other deer spirits that he has been treated well. One finds this way of handling things and animals in all primitive cultures.

THREE POEMS

LAWSON FUSAO INADA

FROM MINE TO YOURS

Enclosed, enraptured
by my own scent and image,
I watch you pass

in yours,
in your own shaft of light.

2

There are things in here
that make me shudder.

I won't tell you about them.

I don't tell myself.

3

Instead, I watch my
outer image—

myself on all sides
paired off with another.

That and my breath
on the glass.

Watch me as you pass.

You make me watch you.

4

It seems all water
finds me.
Each droplet magnifies.

They tell me that I . . .

5

This is what I try
to reach you about,
through all hours of the night.

You in yours,
incoherent, seeping
fear into the receiver . . .

Moist. Hot.

I plunge you to my crotch.

6

Then to find myself
washed up, knocked over,
kicking without consequence
on the shores of streets.

Monopod. Mollusk.

7

Sheathed, stiffened
by the ice-storm—

all reeds in glass.

To be released
by what the frost promises—

patterns that make
the world again.

Nothing new.

Just dunes, ocean,
a cold wind
shattering
ice with a crash.

The sun on all that.

Shall I say
that makes me glad?

What else can I say?

Would you listen if I could?

A RAILROAD SONG

I was up late,
troubling about the trouble
in Czechoslovakia,
So I decided to look it up
in the atlas—

a book so big
you need a podium to hold it,
something to lean on
as you roam each massive page.

The country was there,
so I started to roam . . .

. . . The earth in formation—
how it expanded and cooled;
the earth in cross-section—
skin-surface, the molten core;
the earth and the sun—
a spot on a curve

too huge for the book to hold . . .

All this before
densities, heights,
the major religions . . .

I think I fell asleep
in Clovis, New Mexico—

sun on the station as the p.a. droned . . .

This morning, just
roaming around,
I had to stop for a slowed-down diesel,
then noticed as he picked up speed
all the others behind him.

I started to count and read:

> One Southern Pacific
> two Burlington
> three Southern Pacific
> four Great Northern
> five Southern Pacific
> six Southern Pacific
> seven Rock Island
> eight Southern Pacific
> nine Southern Pacific

faster and faster
until he left me
rocking in his wake
hundred thirty-seven Southern Pacific
waving at a face in the caboose,
cars at back
howling about church,
choiring with the National Guard . . .

I'd have followed to another crossing
but it was long gone
by the time I awoke . . .

Since then, I've been thinking:

on designated days
we could decide upon,
I'd like to meet with friends
in the pearl of morning
at anyone's house,
for coffee and toast.

Maybe others would join us:

the face over a thermos in the caboose;
the face under the welding mask;
the face at the cash register . . .

We could just talk about things—

What we did and saw—

like the big atlas,
like the train . . .

And maybe that would take us
down to the tracks, just to see

What was coming and going;

and maybe we could join

in a railroad song.

A SON IN THE HOUSE

I   LITTLE MILES

My boy is a small
accordion,
a wheeze
and a little trill.

And when I squeeze
him, he sings
high in the upper
register of love.

II OFF AND ON

Off schedule, off
beat, off
the beaten
weekday track
we need, up
at dawn, those
squeamish hours,
we find him
squalling in a
wet wind spinning
the bees of his
crib mobile.

Then dry, a little
daubing. Bubbles
sing in his
mouth like springs.
It is cold
outside, those
high mountains
where the snows
live and die.
We say hello,
hello again
to the world.

III IN THESE TIMES

Lately, my front teeth have been aching,
and my lips are always rough.
The doctor says: "You're laughing too much."

And that's how much I love my only son.

IV   SOMETHING, MAYBE

An unseasonal snow.
Tonight, the return of
red men hunched
in their orchards over
smudge-pots, deciphering
hieroglyphs, the old stories . . .
Smoke curling
darkly, in Arabic.
Bushes, asterisks.
The sky's gray page.

Miles on the rug, munching
a rubber humpty-dumpty.
It's a wonder
he's here:

teaching himself
to crawl—lectures
of ligaments and knees . . .

And what will I say?

Something, maybe,
about the chromosomes
counting their fingers . . .

I don't even know
how this poem got here:

something, maybe,
about computer tape—

feed-in, feed-back . . .

And from the rug it's
another story,
the table's screwed-up tale
about braces, snot,
saying the landlord's a spider . . .

So what can I tell my boy?

I think I'll simply say:

"It is written."

And that plants
wait like commas under the snow.

Read. Enjoy.

ON THE REBOUND

JAMES PURDY

"Frankly, gentlemen," Rupert Douthwaite reflected one gray afternoon in January to a few of us Americans who visited him from
time to time in his "exile" in London, "no one in New York, no one
who counted ever expected to see Georgia Comstock back in town,"
and here Rupert nodded on the name, in his coy pompous but
somewhat charming way, meaning for us to know she was an
heiress, meaning she had "everything," otherwise he would not be
mentioning her. "She sat right there," he pointed to a refurbished
heirloom chair which had accompanied him from New York. "I
would never have dreamed Georgia would sue for a favor, least of
all to me, for, after all," he touched a colorful sideburn, "if you will
allow me to remind you, it was I who replaced Georgia so far as
literary salons were concerned." He groaned heavily, one of his old
affectations, and took out his monocle, one of his new ones, and let
it rest on the palm of his hand like an expiring butterfly. "Georgia's
was, after all, the only bona fide salon in New York for years and
years—I say that, kind friends, without modification. It was never
elegant, never grand, never *comme il faut*, granted, any more than
poor Georgia was. She was plain, mean, and devastating, with her
own consistent vulgarity and bad taste, but she had the energy of
a fiend out of hot oil and she turned that energy into establishing
the one place where everybody had to turn up on a Thursday in
New York, whether he liked it or not.

"When the dear thing arrived, then, at my place after her long
banishment, I was pained to see how much younger she'd gotten.

It didn't become her. I preferred her old, let's say. It was obvious she'd had the finest face-lifting job Europe can bestow. (You know how they've gone all wrong in New York on that. You remember Kathryn Combs, the film beauty. One eye's higher than the other now, dead mouth, and so on, so that I always feel when Kathryn's about I'm looking into an open casket.) But Georgia! Well, she hardly looked forty.

"Now mind you, I knew she hadn't come back to New York to tell me she loved me—the woman's probably hated me all my life, no doubt about it, but whatever she's come for, I had to remind myself she had been helpful when Kitty left me," Rupert referred openly now to his third wife, the great New York female novelist who had walked out on him for, in his words, a shabby little colonel. "Yes," he sighed now, "when all the papers were full of my divorce before I myself hardly knew she had left me, Georgia was most understanding, even kind, moved in to take care of me, hovered over me like a mother bird, and so on. I had been ready to jump in the river, and she, bitch that she is, brought me round. And so when she appeared five years to the day after New York had kicked her out, and with her brand-new face, I saw at once she had come on a matter as crucial to her as my bustup had been with Kitty, but I confess I never dreamed she had come to me because she wanted to begin all over again (begin with a salon, I mean of course). Nobody decent begins again, as I tried to tell her immediately I heard what she was up to. She'd been living in Yugoslavia, you know, after the New York fiasco . . .

"When she said she did indeed want to begin again, I simply replied, 'Georgia, you're not serious and you're not as young as you look either, precious. You can't know what you're saying. Maybe it's the bad New York air that's got you after the wheat fields and haymows of Slavonia.'

" 'Rupert, my angel,' she intoned, 'I'm on my knees to you, and not rueful to be so! Help me to get back and to stay back, dearest!'

" 'Nonsense,' I made her stop her dramatics, 'I won't hear of it, and you won't hear of it either when you're yourself again.'

"I was more upset than I should have been somehow. Her coming and her wish for another try at a salon made me aware what was already in the wind, something wicked that scared me a little, and I heard myself voicing it when I said, 'Everything has changed in New York, sweety, since you've been away. You wouldn't know anybody now. Most of the old writers are too afraid to go out even for a stroll any more, and the new ones, you see, meet only on the parade ground. The salon, dear love, I'm afraid, is through.'

" 'I feel I can begin again, Rupert, darling,' she ignored my speech. 'You know it was everything to me, it's everything now. Don't speak to me of the Yugoslav pure air and haymows.'

"Well, I looked her up and down, and thought about everything. There she was, worth twenty million she'd inherited from her pa's death, and worth another six or seven million from what the movies gave her for her detective novels, for Georgia was, whether you boys remember or not, a novelist in her own right. Yet here she was, a flood of grief. I've never seen a woman want anything so much, and in my day I've seen them with their tongues hanging for just about everything.

" 'Let me fix you a nice tall frosty drink like they don't have in Zagreb, angel, and then I'm going to bundle you up and send you home to bed.' But she wouldn't be serious. 'Rupert, my love, if as you said I saved you once (she overstated of course) you've got to save me now.'

"She had come to the heart of her mission.

" 'What did I do wrong before, will you tell me,' she brought out after a brief struggle with pride. 'Why was I driven out of New York, my dear boy. Why was I black-listed, why was every door slammed in my face.' She gave a short sob.

" 'Georgia, my sweet, if you don't know why you had to leave New York, nobody can tell you.' I was a bit abrupt.

" 'But I don't, Rupert!' She was passionate. 'Cross my heart,' she moaned. 'I don't.'

"I shook my finger at her.

" 'You sit there, dear Douthwaite, like the appointed monarch of all creation whose only burden is to say No to all mortal pleas.' She laughed a little, then added, 'Don't be needlessly cruel, you beautiful thing.'

" 'I've never been that,' I told her. 'Not cruel. But, Georgia, you know what you did, and said, the night of your big fiasco, after which oblivion moved in on you. You burned every bridge, highway, and cowpath behind you when you attacked the Negro novelist Burleigh Jordan in front of everybody who matters on the literary scene.'

" 'I? Attacked him?' she scoffed.

" 'My God, you can't pretend you don't remember.' I studied her new mouth and chin. 'Burleigh's grown to even greater importance since *you* left, Georgia. First he was the greatest black writer, then he was the greatest Black, and now, God knows what he is, I've not kept hourly track. But when you insulted him that night, though your ruin was already in the air, it was the end for you, and nearly the end for all of us. I had immediately to go to work to salvage my own future.'

" 'Ever the master of overstatement, dear boy,' she sighed.

"But I was stonyfaced.

" 'So you mean what you say?' she whined, after daubing an eye.

" 'I mean only this, Georgia,' I said emphasizing the point in question. 'I took over when you destroyed yourself,' (and I waited to let it sink in that my own salon, which had been so tiny when Georgia's had been so big, had been burgeoning while she was away, and had now more than replaced her. I was *her* now, in a manner of speaking).

" 'Supposing then you tell me straight out what I said to Burleigh.' She had turned her back on me while she examined a new painting I had acquired as a matter of fact only a day or so before. I could tell she didn't think much of it, for she turned from it almost at once.

" 'Well?' she prompted me.

" 'Oh, don't expect me to repeat your exact words after all the water has flowed under the bridge since you said them. Your words were barbarous, of course, but it was your well-known tone of voice, as well as the exquisitely snotty timing of what you said, that did the trick. You are the empress of all bitches, darling, and if you wrote books as stabbing as you talk you'd have no peer . . . You said in four or five different rephrasings of your original affidavit, that you would never kiss a black ass if it meant you and your Thursdays were to be ground to powder.'

" 'Oh, I completely disremember such a droll statement,' she giggled.

"Just then the doorbell rang, and in came four or five eminent writers, all of whom were surprised to see Georgia, and Georgia could not mask her own surprise that they were calling on me so casually. We rather ignored her then, but she wouldn't leave, and when they found the bottles and things, and were chattering away, Georgia pushed herself among us, and began on me again.

"At last more to get rid of her than anything else, I proposed to her the diabolic, unfeasible scheme which I claimed would reinstate her everywhere, pave the way for the reopening of her Thursday salon. I am called everywhere the most soulless cynic who ever lived, but I swear by whatever any of you hold holy, if you ever hold anything, that I never dreamed she would take me on when I said to her that all she'd be required to do was give Burleigh the token kiss she'd said she never would, to make it formal and she'd be back in business. You see I thought she would leave in a huff when she heard my innocent proposal and that in a few days New York would see her no more—at least I'd be rid of her. Well, say she'd quaffed one too many of my frosty master-pieces, say again it was the poisonous New York air, whatever, I stood dumbfounded when I heard her say simply, "Then make it next Thursday, darling, and I'll be here, and tell Burleigh not to fail us, for I'll do it, Rupert darling, I'll do it for you, I'll do it for all of us.'

"The next day I rang to tell her of course that she wasn't to take me seriously, that my scheme had been mere persiflage, etc. She simply rang off after having assured me the deal was on and she'd be there Thursday.

"I was so angry with the bitch by then I rang up big black Burleigh and simply, without a word of preparation, told him. You see, Burleigh and I were more than friends at that time, let's put it that way," Rupert smirked a bit with his old self-assurance, "and," he went on, "to my mild surprise perhaps, the dear lion agreed to the whole thing with alacrity.

"After a few hours of sober reflection, I panicked. I called Burleigh back first and tried to get him not to come. But Burleigh was at the height of a new wave of paranoia and idol-worship and he could do no wrong. He assured me he wanted to come, wanted to go through with our scheme, which he baptized divine. I little knew then of course how well he had planned to go through with it, and neither of course did poor Georgia!

"Then of course I tried again to get Georgia not to come. It was like persuading Joan of Arc to go back to her livestock. I saw everything coming then the way it did come, well, not *everything*," here he looked wistfully around at the London backdrop and grinned, for he missed New York even more when he talked about it, and he hadn't even the makings of a salon in London of course, though he'd made a stab at it.

"I didn't sleep the night before," Rupert Douthwaite went on to describe the event to which he owed his ruin. "I thought I was daring, I thought I had always been in advance of everything—after all, *my* Thursdays had been at least a generation ahead of Georgia's in smartness, taste and éclat, and now, well, as I scented the fume-heavy air, somebody was about to take the lead over from me.

"Everybody came that night—wouldn't you know it, some people from Washington, a tiresome princess or so, and indeed all the crowned heads from all the avenues of endeavor managed to get there, as if they sensed what was to come off. There was even that fat man from Kansas City who got himself circumcised a few seasons back to make the literary scene in New York.

"Nobody recognized Georgia at first when she made her entrance, not even Burleigh. She was radiant, if slightly drawn, and for the first time I saw that her face-lifting job wasn't quite stress-proof, but still she only looked half her age, and so she was a howling success at first blush.

" 'Now, my lovely,' I spoke right into her ear redolent of 200-dollar-an-ounce attar of something, 'please bow to everybody and then go home—my car is downstairs parked directly by the door, Wilson is at the wheel. You've made a grand hit tonight, and go now while they're all still cheering.'

" 'I'm going through with it, love,' she was adamant, and I saw Burleigh catch the old thing's eye and wink.

" 'Not in my house, you won't,' I whispered to her, kissing her again and again in deadly desperation to disguise my murderous expression from the invited guests. 'After all,' I repeated, 'my little scheme was proposed while we were both in our cups.'

" 'And it's in cups where the truth resides, Douthwaite, as the Latin proverb has it,' and she kissed me on the lips and left me, walking around the room as in her old salon grandeur days, grasping everybody's outstretched hand, letting herself be embraced and kissed. She was a stunning dizzy success, and then suddenly I felt that neither she nor Burleigh had any intention of doing what they had agreed to do. I was the fool who had fallen for their trap.

"When I saw what a hit she was making, I took too many drinks, for the more accolades she got, the angrier and more disturbed I became. I wasn't going to let Georgia come back and replace me, whatever else might happen.

"I went over to where Burleigh was being worshipped to death.

He turned immediately to me to say, 'Don't you come over here, Ruppie, to ask me again not to do what I am sure as greased lightning I'm going to do, baby' and he smiled his angry smile at me.

" 'Burleigh, dearest,' I took him by the hand, 'I not only want you to go through with it bigger and grander but megatons more colossal than we had planned. That's the message I have to give you,' and I kissed and hugged him quietly.

"I couldn't be frightened now, and what I had just proposed to him was a little incredible even for me, even for me drunk, I had gone all out I dimly realized, and asked for an assassination.

"But the more I saw Georgia's success with everybody, the more I wanted the horror that was going to happen. And then there was the size of her diamond. It was too much. No one wore diamonds that big in the set we moved in. She did it to hurt me, to show me up to the others, that whereas I might scrape up a million, let's say, she had so much money she couldn't add it all up short of two years of auditing.

"Time passed. I looked in the toilet where Burleigh was getting ready, and hugged encouragement.

"Then I felt the great calm people are said to feel on learning they have but six months to live. I gave up, got the easiest seat and the one nearest to the stage, and collapsed. People forgot me.

"Still the hog of the scene, Georgia was moving right to where she knew she was to give her comeback performance.

"Some last minute celebrities had just come in, to whom I could only barely nod, a duchess, and some minor nobility, a senator, a diva, and somehow from somewhere a popular film critic of the hour who had discovered he was not homosexual, when with a boom and a guffaw Burleigh sails out of the john wearing feathers on his head but otherwise not a stitch on him.

"I saw Georgia freeze ever so slightly—you see in our original scheme nothing was said about nakedness, it was all, in any case, to have been a token gesture, she had thought—indeed *I* had thought, but she stopped, put down her glass, squared her shoul-ders like a good soldier, and waited.

"Burleigh jumped up on my fine old walnut table cleared for the occasion. Everybody pretended to like it. Georgia began to weave around like a rabbit facing a python. Burleigh turned his back to her, and bent over, and with a war hoop extended his black biscuits to her. She stood reeling, waiting for the long count, then I heard, rather than saw, owing to heads in the way, her kissing his behind, then rising I managed to see him proffer his front and middle to her, everything there waving, when someone blotted out my view again, but I gathered from the murmur of the crowd she had gone through with it, and kissed his front too.

"Then I heard her scream, and I got up in time to see that Burleigh had smeared her face with some black tarlike substance and left a few of his white turkey feathers over that.

"I believe Georgia tried to pretend she had wanted this last too, and that it was all a grand charade, but her screams belied it, and she and Burleigh stood facing one another like victims of a car accident.

"It had all failed, I realized immediately. Everybody was sickened or bored. Nothing was a success about it. Call it wrong timing, wrong people, wrong actors or hour of the evening, oh explain it any way you will, it was all ghastly and cruddy with nonsuccess.

"I stumbled over to the back of my apartment, and feeling queasy, lay down on the floor near the rubber plant. I thought queerly of Kitty who had, it seemed, just left me, and I—old novelist *manqué*—thought of all those novels I had written which publishers never even finished reading in typescript, let alone promised to publish, and I gagged loudly. People bent down to me and seemed to take my pulse, and then others began filing out, excusing themselves by a cough or nod, or stifling a feeble giggle. They thought I had fainted from chagrin. They thought I had not planned it. They thought I was innocent but ruined.

"I have never seen such a clean, wholesale, bloody failure. Like serving a thin warm soup and calling it Baked Alaska.

"I didn't see anybody for weeks. Georgia, I understand, left for Prague a few days later. Only Burleigh was not touched by anything. Nothing can harm him, bad reviews, public derision, all he has to do is clap his hands, and crowds hoist him on their shoulders, the money falls like rain in autumn.

"Burleigh has his own salon now, if you can call his big gatherings on Saturday a salon, and Georgia and I both belong to a past more remote than the French and Indian Wars.

"To answer your first question, Gordon," Rupert turned now to me, for I was his favorite American of the moment, "I've found London quieting, yes, but it's not my world exactly, sweety, since I'm not in or of it, but that's what I need, isn't it, to sit on the side lines for a season and enjoy a statelier backdrop? I don't quite know where Georgia is. Somebody says it's Bulgaria."

SOME POEMS FOR MAX ERNST

ROBERT BLY

TRAIN WRECK IN MIDOCEAN

Night sea. High waves. The train is falling off the trestle!
Murderous sea. Waves that adore empty
husks and exhausted pianos.

The train is arching Off! Near the
Newfoundland Banks. A huge and sardonic
Woman stands looking down.
Just before dawn, the whole Burlington train
   will go back into her belly button, but now
the screams have to go on,
   the mashed shoulders,
the passengers with faces pressed to the window!

Black insects go mad in their sleep,
Flames dance just over the water.

Monks kneel
in the Shang mounds long since destroyed
muttering all night "The Song of the Mountain Mother."

SCENE WITH RESPECTABLE MEN

Here are two portly men.
The inhabitants of muskrat marshes have come to visit one.
There is a marten climbing up his leg.
A wingéd man comes near.
He wears bourgeois wings, good only for flying over low houses,
or rising from table.
Their fingers point to a Paradise of paracedic bottles,
heavens of intestines, of testaments left
in dog bowls, bowls of water set out for the dead—
the dead are now Australian sloths, panting, thirsty, on the
        edges of ice floes.

COLLAPSING BRIDGE

Whenever a bridge falls,
you can be sure a naked woman has been sleeping beside it.
It *is* just
that women live longer than men!
Thousands of small men topple off the bridge, dropping
into the water
        glassy, acquarious, cunning with undercurrents—
How sadly the cables hang!
as the French Revolution ends.

SMALL SCENE WITH WINGÉD MAN

She opens a door—and there he is!
How long it takes for the two hands to touch!
He has a drinking hand, that has stuffed
Bibles at midnight
into greasy overcoat pockets.
She has a hand that loses things.
His black wings are half open over the snow.

MOTHER COMING

Yes, now I see my mother coming!
Murdered men hang out of the trees.
Infant tornadoes go by, whirling, the Virgin glowing
      in the center, like a bulb.
A man rolls his hands.
Black discs sweep elegantly by over the far trees.
Mother, come live inside one of my teeth!
I will make you a root-table, and rough wooden chairs
to sit by the fire.
I will eat, then clean the black altar joyfully.
Genghis Khan can come along then, on the altar,
the small shaggy horses furry with frost.
We will sit in a city that turns blue and then explodes.

READING OLD BOOKS

Go on then, hide from the world!
It doesn't matter—the spidery seas
run up your leg, typhoons
carry away the holes in your mother's head,
the smallest will buckles, your knee
touches the floor by the failed bed,
I weep, heads drift
down, what's the difference?
It is the seas that no one can end,
private bays the mariners spun around
in, their green ships crushed
by wallocky rocks,
insane Mary, you've gone to save
the muddy seafloor, snails come out to accompany us,
we will never be lonely.

FOR MY FATHER

You are like the Sphinx looking at me, father!
It is no use to turn away!
Kesselring will come, and the cicadas
will sing at night in the camaranth trees.
Turkey feathers
all gathered together in the duster,
rustling in the open window.
The window is open.

Rolling seas, seething with ice, lift
all night the black ships.
We are lying, the two of us,
like black seals on the ice floes.

TURTLE CLIMBING FROM A ROCK

How beautiful the shiny turtle is, coming out
of the water, on the rock, as if
Buddha's spirit were to shine!
As if swift turtle wings swept out of darkness,
crossed the barriers,
and found new eyes.
The old man falters with his stick,
later, walkers find holes in black earth.
The snail climbs up the wet trunk shining
like an angel-flight trailing long black banners.
No one finds the huge turtle eggs
lying inland on the floor of the old sea.

GIBBON'S BODY

Night goes by . . . nightwheels are rushing by outside,
throwing fragments of Gibbon's body to the light-hawks.
It's no use . . . the mind is overjoyed at its own absence
          of concentration.
It runs over the earth, its tongue a quarter inch from the dust.
Friends collapsing, eating the cobalt of spilled milk,
Death to caterpillars—evil thoughts cause saliva to run
          from the cow's tongue,
orphans stagger giving out starlight sounds when they hit trees.
Children wrapped in blue moss fly over the horrible cities.
The third-rate violinist suddenly plays like Menuhin.

TO THE READER

It's raining in the immense room on the other side of the womb,
where the dead gibber, waving their white canes like hands.

Bubbles ooze from the ground,
mouths open and close to make day and night,
we sleep there, in the translucent bladder of the porgy.

KETCHUP

A Play In Five Parts

RUSSELL EDSON

The Characters: Father and Mother, stout and middle-aged. Their two sons, Percival and Oscar, men in their thirties.

I

FATHER. I'm afraid a rather dangerous situation has developed between ourselves and the neighbors. As I was moving from one point to another, in my usual attempt to process myself through the efficiency that the shortest distance between two points is a straight line; I was returning from the office to our lovely home. But luck ran out. What served as the habit of the years, the to and fro of my coming and going, save Sundays and other holidays, has come to an abrupt and unseemly end . . .

MOTHER. Oh Father, Father, what cruel thing have you brought upon us?

FATHER. I stepped on the neighbor's child. It lay in my path. I calculated: Will I be able to avoid it? No, it seemed that I would not. Perhaps I shall be able to step over it? Confusion and doubt grew strong in me. As a high jumper paces his stride to the bar . . . No, as I drew upon the child I saw that it was too late. One of my beautiful English oxfords went squarely on the child. I feared that I might slip . . .

MOTHER. It can be dangerous.

FATHER. The neighbors started to run after me. Now I increased my gait. I was running.

MOTHER. Oh Father, at your age that's a dangerous thing.

FATHER. However, the male neighbor seemed more threat than the exertion to remove myself from the immediate range of his operation.

MOTHER. Good thinking, Father.

FATHER. Thank you, my dear. We shall of course have to close the shutters on the windows . . .

MOTHER. But my beautiful curtains. When people pass the house they say the woman has beautiful curtains, she must be a beautiful woman . . .

FATHER. Hard times. And we shall have to build a dummy and fill it with ketchup. We'll put it out at night in the yard so the male neighbor will have something to vent his anger on.

MOTHER. Not all my home-bottled ketchup? No, that is too cruel. How can I eat beans and steak? What will spinach taste like without ketchup?

FATHER. Hard times. I must contribute my best suit to the dummy.

MOTHER. Why should the dummy demand all our things?

FATHER. It is a sacrifice, and gives its life for mine. Dare we do less for one who is to be the victim of the male neighbor?

MOTHER. Perhaps if you apologize on the telephone . . . ?

FATHER. He might hang up on me.

MOTHER. Rudeness is unforgivable.

FATHER. Hard times, people become rude.

MOTHER. And our children, how shall they grow up to be useful citizens?

FATHER. They'll have to give it up.

MOTHER. Give up what?

FATHER. Growing up, or becoming useful citizens. They can't do both. Hard times teach us that what we took for granted never took us so.

MOTHER. And they so wanted to be useful citizens . . .

FATHER. Well, Mother, in a country as rich as this they can still get along without being useful.

MOTHER. Perhaps you could go to the male neighbor and offer yourself in place of his child.

FATHER. No, Mother, it's not dignified. Even in hard times one must maintain a certain dignity.

MOTHER. Of course, Father; and I think it was a girl child, anyway. I think you would have been the wrong sex.

FATHER. Why do you bring up sex at a time like this?

MOTHER. I only meant . . .

FATHER. That's the trouble with you, you speak before you think.

MOTHER. But, Father, I only meant . . .

FATHER. That's exactly the trouble with you. Now that we have come upon hard times, more than ever, we need to stick together. And what do you do . . . ?

MOTHER. Oh, Father, what shall we do?

FATHER. As our energies permit, we must bring all our resources to play. The house must be made into a fort. We shall say our prayers before bedtime, regularly. Not that I place much benefit to this procedure; but there's no use in missing out on a protective measure by being too smart. It's dangerous to be too smart.

MOTHER. Oh Father, it is smart not to be too smart.

FATHER. Don't get smart with me.

MOTHER. I only meant . . .

FATHER. That's the trouble with you, you talk before you think. Before you apply any moral censorship your mouth is open and the foulest implications are falling out of it.

MOTHER. But Father . . .

FATHER. But Father nothing; enough of these excuses and dodges. If you cannot see the extreme danger to our house because of the male neighbor, not to mention his wife, the female neighbor . . . How do I know they have not got relatives scattered around the neighborhood, placed in such positions that they could not attack the house from all directions? My God, and you want to talk about sex. What on earth could sex mean to me at a time like this, or at my age? My God, you haven't talked about sex for twenty years. Why now?—Just as I am trying to save the house . . .

MOTHER. Why are you yelling at me? Did I step on the neighbor's child? Did I set the male neighbor against you? You did these things, and now you yell at me, expecting my loyalty . . .

FATHER. Mother, forgive me; you can see I'm quite nervous . . .

MOTHER. Of course, my dear . . . And, after all, being a useful citizen isn't everything; surely being an unuseful citizen must have some use . . .

FATHER. How can being unuseful be useful? Do you see how you attack, how you whittle down my mental energies . . . ?

MOTHER. I only meant . . .

FATHER. You see, you see, again you only meant . . . Why do you make me fight you; you know that I'm at odds with the world . . . Why are you so disloyal?

MOTHER. I was only trying to rationalize a situation being forced on our children; after all, they've spent their whole lives looking forward to being useful citizens . . .

FATHER. Hard times, Mother, hard times . . .

MOTHER. And whose fault?

FATHER. See, you're accusing me!

MOTHER. Well, you see, the children did want to be useful citizens, which would have made me the mother of useful citizens; a very useful mother. But, as it is now all we can hope for is the preservation of our lives. And since we are getting old and shall lose them anyway, what is the use?

FATHER. Oh, so you *are* blaming me.

MOTHER. What good is it to blame; what's done is done.

FATHER. You blame so you can find the wound. So you can say, there, that is the hurtful spot, that is the injury. The mind rests easier when it finds the object of its disquiet.

MOTHER. Hush, Father, you're about to say something ugly.

FATHER. Does it occur to you that the male neighbor is stronger than I am; that he will run right over me and rape you?

MOTHER. Which is his right.

FATHER. What right has he to rape you?

MOTHER. The right of the victor.

FATHER. Are you turning?

MOTHER. But is there any necessity to use all my homemade ketchup?

FATHER. Is there any question about its use if it decoys away the blow meant for me?

MOTHER. But you know how I hate spinach without ketchup.

FATHER. Do you understand that I want to use the ketchup instead of my own blood?

MOTHER. But Father, you have your own blood, why do you want to involve the ketchup?

FATHER. Because ketchup is less dear than blood.

MOTHER. I worked so hard to put the ketchup up.

FATHER. Would you rather my blood to the ketchup?

MOTHER. Now that's silly; of course not. It's just that I don't want you to ruin my ketchup just for spite.

FATHER. Shut up, you do not understand me.

MOTHER. Perhaps if you went to the male neighbor and apologized . . .

FATHER. Apologize. Are you crazy? Something wrong with your head? I'd have about as much dignity left as yesterday's fashions. In hard times one has only his dignity . . . *(A rock comes through the window.)* It's begun. At this time I wish to make a statement . . .

MOTHER. Yes, say something . . . Just look at the window.

FATHER. A state of war exists between ourselves and those who inhabit the adjoining property. As your leader, I call upon the members of this household to have courage, and to remember that blood is thicker than ketchup . . .

MOTHER. No it's not, Father.

FATHER. Never mind, every war has its slogan.

MOTHER. Look, Father, there's a note tied to the rock.

FATHER. *(He picks up the rock.)* Maybe they wish to surrender . . .

MOTHER. What does it say?

FATHER. It asks for our unconditional surrender . . .

MOTHER. What does that mean?

FATHER. Oh shut up!

II

(The house is in shambles, their clothes are torn.)

FATHER. Where's the dummy?

MOTHER. *(from off stage)* I'm bringing it. *(She drags it on to the stage.)*

FATHER. That's not me.

MOTHER. No no, nor was it meant to be, no more than you were meant to be in the beginning . . .

FATHER. No no, it flatters nothing; nor does it extend by any means native luck, the indigenous resplendency . . .

MOTHER. It's stuffed with brassieres and women's drawers and enema bags of ketchup, rubber prophylactics full of ketchup, children's balloons full of ketchup; all the token gut of a man.

FATHER. That's not me.

MOTHER. Nor is it meant more than any of us in the endless repetition.

FATHER. Without flattery.

MOTHER. Without insult.

FATHER. There is no middle ground. If without flattery it insults.

MOTHER. It is a victim.

FATHER. Oh, I see. Not that I do the act, but that I deliver him who is done the act, so am I guilty . . .

MOTHER. Guilt? It is to be seen as the tumblers in a lock, each falling through a predicted portion; each event upon a single axle falls predicted, and the lock falls free and the future swings out, and you see as through an open door . . .

FATHER. No no, I wish only to study an interior of walls. No no, I have no wish for doors. If one is guilty he wishes only to look at wallpaper. In wallpaper are things right. There the milkmaid and all her sisters bear yokes of milk through the facsimile summer. One would give long periods of life to wondering about the happenings behind the doorframe where the wallpaper disappears. There naked milkmaids have put down their yokes, and roll about in the grass of the facsimile summer, revealing those parts which differ markedly from equally luscious boys . . . And to spend days thusly, in so refusing else than this . . .

MOTHER. But Father, the male neighbor grows great with wrath, and practices your death a thousand times . . .

FATHER. Of course he does. He always did. Does not any neighbor practice the death of his neighbor? Does not any neighbor given right by the act of his neighbor, rejoice that he is given vent?

MOTHER. Oh Father, you make the world so terrible.

FATHER. Why do you turn against me in the moment of crisis, just when your love is at greatest premium . . . when, without it I have only myself, which I cannot find; though I search myself I cannot find myself. In all memory I see only events peopled by others; and I cannot find myself. Mother, where am I?

MOTHER. Dear, look, the milkmaids; one learns a certain bravery there. They look not to the future, nor do they look out of the past, but in the moment that is the lifetime of a family, they carry milk up the hill to that little house. One knows not what awaits them there . . . If, in fact, the walls are not covered with milkmaids also carrying milk to even smaller houses, which too have a wallpaper of milkmaids . . .

FATHER. Oh stop it! Is the male neighbor not mad enough now? Surely enough time has passed to where the boilers of his anger must be near to bursting.

MOTHER. Well, put the dummy outside.

FATHER. Is it night yet?

MOTHER. Do you have eyes?

FATHER. Why are you talking fresh?

MOTHER. I'm sorry; every so often I despise you.

FATHER. Just when I need your love.

MOTHER. I try to hide it, but every so often . . .

FATHER. Again I stand alone; whoever I am I stand alone . . .

MOTHER. Oh Father, I'm standing right next to you.

FATHER. Not really; even I have run away from myself. I should put myself out in the yard instead of the dummy.

MOTHER. It's getting dark.

FATHER. (He takes the dummy under its arms and drags it to the door.) I suppose it's time to put the dummy out.

MOTHER. Poor thing . . .

FATHER. Would you rather I put myself out?

MOTHER. Make it comfortable.

FATHER. It's not alive.

MOTHER. No, I suppose not.

FATHER. You suppose?

MOTHER. Don't press me, Father.

FATHER. Press you?

MOTHER. Go along, don't make it any harder than it is.

FATHER. What is hard about putting a decoy out to save your husband's life?

MOTHER. I've heard enough; just put it out!

(The Father drags the dummy out of the door.)

III

(Several weeks have passed; the house is restored. They are no longer wearing torn clothing.)

MOTHER. Is the peace difficult?

FATHER. Not when one remembers the difficulty of war.

MOTHER. But one forgets, getting further and further away from the hardship.

FATHER. It's unpatriotic not to remember the dead, and the sacrifices of the living.

MOTHER. Is the peace difficult?

FATHER. I just said it shouldn't be.

MOTHER. But if the glands be still at the ready . . .

FATHER. Be quiet!

MOTHER. But the glands . . .

FATHER. Let them sweat!

MOTHER. But if the heart is not ready to conclude its expectations?

FATHER. Expectations?

MOTHER. That heavy thumping that irrigates and nourishes the hand . . .

FATHER. What hand? What are you talking about?

MOTHER. Is the peace difficult, Father?

FATHER. You are making it difficult.

MOTHER. Will the children be able to become useful citizens?

FATHER. Is there no rest?

MOTHER. Life is a stream.

FATHER. Shut up! The war is over. The male neighbor is in repose.

MOTHER. Can things ever be as they were?

FATHER. Mother, Mother, these questions . . . Realistically, things can never be the same; but one must hope for another path equally complacent as the one destroyed by the war, equally as thoughtless and comfortable as before the war. The best men has is that they die in their own beds while dreaming of confections . . .

MOTHER. But the children, they want the illusion of usefulness.

FATHER. Damn them. Each man for himself. That they decorate the household, it is well. But should they rise in expectations that weigh upon me, falling from decorative amusement, I turn a valve in my heart and cast them from my sympathies.

MOTHER. Our children . . .

FATHER. . . . Not more than any of the others who disturb me. No, Mother, I have found nothing in this life that recommends any allegiance, or the remission of self-concern in lieu of another. We get through as best as we can, as it were, in a pattern unconcerned with us. Each man is a boundary, a distant land . . . Men attempt to perpetuate with pyramids and sons . . . The lies that men call history . . . Codes of honor, custom . . .

MOTHER. If the children should hear they would have preferred that you died in the war; that they might remember their brave papa . . .

FATHER. What do I care for their preferences? Don't you understand; the male neighbor thinks he has killed me. I am now a prisoner of the house. I can never be seen again in public.

MOTHER. Isn't there some way to get the male neighbor gradually used to you? You might introduce a piece of your dandruff in his path, then a hair, or a fingernail; slowly, but surely, easing yourself into his awareness . . .

FATHER. No no, Mother . . . Even if it should work he should always have it on me that I killed his child. No no, it would be too embarrassing. He could always bring it up in his conversation. He could ask to borrow my golf clubs, and could I say no? Don't you see the disadvantage of it? It is too compromising, it would make me too vulnerable . . .

MOTHER. Always thinking of yourself . . .

FATHER. Mother, please, I shall need every pleasant distraction . . .

MOTHER. And to think I gave up all my ketchup for this . . .

FATHER. I shall need to think pleasant thoughts. I shall need to be told over and over again that I acted in the family interest. You and the children will have to think up amusements, just as though you were caring for an incurable invalid . . .

MOTHER. No no, you will have to call the male neighbor up and tell him that it was all a mistake. No no, you cannot expect us to accept the inward life; the children are most taken with saluting flags. No no, they have plans to join the Rotary Club, and the Junior Chamber of Commerce. They have been tying knots all week preparing to join the Boy Scouts, with a view of entering business . . .

FATHER. War munitions; my advice is for them to place their money on munitions, always an excellent return . . . But, they must remember not to antagonize their neighbors; take it from me, I think I have a pretty good idea about community relations. And they mustn't masturbate, that's strictly a kid's game . . .

MOTHER. Oh Father, do you think . . . ?

FATHER. I do, indeed . . . All they need to do is learn how to tie knots and smile . . .

MOTHER. . . . Tie knots and smile . . . Oh Father, call up the male neighbor and tell him it was all a mistake.

FATHER. He might just take that opportunity to insult me . . .

MOTHER. Oh Father, try.

FATHER. Well . . . No, he might insult me, he has every justification on his side; it's too compromising . . . *(telephone rings.)* Don't answer it; it's him, he must be reading our thoughts . . . *(The telephone continues to ring.)*

MOTHER. We've got to answer it, if only to keep the bell from wearing out. *(The telephone continues ringing.)*

FATHER. If we answer it we shall be compromised. *(The telephone continues.)*

MOTHER. Father, please, it's giving me a headache. Phones always make me feel like going to the bathroom. *(Telephone continues.)*

FATHER. *(He picks up the receiver)* . . . Local Scoutmaster? Why yes, indeed, you people do a fine job with our boys; how lovely of you to invite my boys to join. They've been practicing the tying of knots; and they have very winning smiles . . . What was that? . . . Your young daughter . . . viciously run down by your neighbor? . . . Did you ever think that it might have been a mistake? . . . The deed was bigger than the motive . . . Well, that's one way of looking at it; however, the courts take into account the difference between premeditation and accident. No, indeed, I have no wish to defend this vicious crime. It is indefensible. I quite agree with you, he should be drawn and quartered . . . But, but, think of his wife and family; surely, if he has any sons they would want to join the Boy Scouts; you won't keep them out just because of that? . . . Even if they had winning smiles . . . ? How about knot tying, every Scoutmaster is a sucker for knot tying . . . Not even knot tying? . . . Well, here's something, the boys love to salute things; they really go for dedicating themselves in public . . . to anything

. . . Then the Rotary Club and the Junior Chamber of Commerce are out, too? . . . Well, listen, supposing the murderer was willing to fill in for your little girl, a kind of substitute child. Yes, he would wear little dresses and curtsy; he could have ring curls on the side of his head, he's bald on top . . . No, I realize it's not the same thing, the sexual difference in the grown man is too obvious; body hair is disgusting on little girls . . . Well, it certainly is a problem . . . But, it does seem a shame that the lives of the boys should be spoiled because their father had a little accident . . . Oh, yes, I quite understand . . . In your place I should feel . . . But, of course . . . You wouldn't be human . . Any red-blooded . . . My very thoughts, his wife should be raped, and his sons run out of town on a rail . . . So glad you called. Good-bye . . .

IV

(The sons, Percival and Oscar, grown men, dressed as Boy Scouts, are standing at attention and occasionally saluting, with smiling reverent faces looking, as if into the future, with upright patriotism.)

FATHER. He knew it was me. He threatened me in the third person. And I do wish those two would practice their patriotic zeal in private.

MOTHER. What are you saying?

FATHER. Their faces seem so empty of late.

MOTHER. They're looking toward the future. They see stocks and bonds . . . We represent a humble beginning. A log cabin, so to speak . . .

FATHER. Log cabin? This is one of the best houses on the block.

MOTHER. It's all symbolic. Think of us as humble peasants. We have a humble faith in the land. We don't quite understand our sons. Fate has a brilliant future in store for them. We noticed that as children they were saluting things. One night we found little Oscar standing at attention in his crib. Percival's first words were, Down with the Communists . . .

FATHER. What has all this to do with my being threatened on the telephone?

MOTHER. The boys proved early to be more than a match for ordinary tasks. Oscar was splitting rails at six months. Percival built the very cabin he was born in . . .

FATHER. Meanwhile the telephone was invented, and their poor humble father became the victim of cruel threats over it . . .

MOTHER. Why do you insist on stealing their glory by interjecting yourself . . .

FATHER. But, you are making it all up . . .

MOTHER. Your highness, your holinesses, what do you attribute your unparalleled success to? A keen interest in anti-Communism, and an undying loyalty to personal ambition . . . And then the applause . . . Father, it's deafening . . .

FATHER. What are you saying?

MOTHER. The boys, they have reached the highest approval. Great minds are met to create new offices for the boys to fill. Countries give up their boundaries that they might merge into one country to be led by our boys. Our boys climb Mt. Everest. Our boys join a circus and become water carriers. Their greatest triumph comes in flagpole sitting . . . Oh, the crowds, the milling, admiring crowds. A petition is gotten up, everyone on earth signs it, asking God not ever to let the boys die. Do you see it, from humble beginnings, a stable in Bethlehem, a log cabin in Kentucky, from a New York tenement, born of immigrant parents, the boys, the boys, sitting under a bo tree, suckled by a wolf, bringing spaghetti back from China—all from humble beginnings, from my log cabin womb, built by their hands, no place at the inn . . .

FATHER. They were both born in a hospital . . .

MOTHER. It's symbolic. They were not like other children. One could tell that they were destined for greatness. Take Oscar, for instance, he was able at his birth to speak with the doctor. Percival assisted at his own birth . . .

FATHER. Shut up. Do you think I want to hear about them while my life is in ruins? You only compound my difficulties with these descriptions which promote a most unflattering comparison . . .

MOTHER. The boys were hampered by a jealous father, who used scorn and humiliation to inhibit their rising expectations. Their father was an alcoholic and a spendthrift. Their poor mother was forced to support the family, and has, fortunately, come to equal enshrinement with her most noteworthy sons. The father was a child molester, and a vicious Communist . . .

FATHER. What are you saying? I am the victim of the Industrial Revolution.

MOTHER. Their father was in a Commy-backed labor union . . .

FATHER. That's a lie! Their father became the victim of Alexander Graham Bell . . .

MOTHER. In revolutionary times their father worked with the British; but the boys crossed the Delaware and won the war against the English Bolsheviks. Their father then joined the great Indian uprising, just as the boys were going West in covered wagons . . .

FATHER. I'm not against the boys . . .

MOTHER. Their father was not a Communist; but he was soft on Communists, he was a Communist dupe . . .

FATHER. The boys are very accomplished, and I mean to take nothing away from them . . . But, it's just possible that the war might start again any minute . . . (A rock comes through the window.)

MOTHER. Oh, why did you have to kill the neighbor's child, she never did anything to you?

FATHER. Mother, it was an accident. You know it was an accident. You gave up all your ketchup because you believed in me . . .

MOTHER. But it's unfair; why should we have to suffer on account of you? The male neighbor wants you, not us. Why should we have to suffer broken windows?

FATHER. But I didn't break the window.

MOTHER. The male neighbor breaks the window instead of you; it's you he wishes to break. It isn't fair. I didn't marry you to live in a house of broken windows. I thought I would be a queen, carried about on a lift-chair; attended to, perfumed, bathed in scented oils; adored, worshipped. No, instead of bouquets, rocks are tossed through the window. You cannot expect me to go on without being worshipped. I haven't been worshipped in all the time I've been married. Look, there's a note tied to the rock.

FATHER. Don't read it . . .

MOTHER. (She picks up the note.) It says . . .

FATHER. No.

MOTHER. It says: one pound of coffee, ten tablespoons, a dozen oranges, toothpicks, if not gold, wooden, a lady's diamond watch, a bottle of aspirin, one pound of chopped meat, a bag of onions, wrinkle cream, and . . .

FATHER. What does it say?

MOTHER. Seven bottles of ketchup, one dust mop, and call the man about fixing the corkscrew . . .

FATHER. What does it mean?

MOTHER. Why do you ask for meaning at a time like this?

FATHER. Because it may make the difference . . .

MOTHER. Of what?

FATHER. Between alternatives.

MOTHER. Father, stop it, stop it, I can't stand any more . . .

FATHER. Perhaps it's a list of reparations, which would make right the breach in our relations; which was caused by an unfortunate accident, leading to a rather dangerous situation having developed between ourselves and the neighbors. Perhaps you've heard of the difficulty . . . ?

MOTHER. No, Father, what is it?

FATHER. You must know what I'm talking about, it's been discussed in the house for quite some time now; surely you've put two and two together . . . ?

MOTHER. What?

FATHER. I stepped on the neighbor's child. It lay in my path. I calculated, will I be able to avoid it? No . . .

MOTHER. Oh that. Yes, I've heard some talk . . .

FATHER. See, I know you must have heard something.

MOTHER. Well, I couldn't help overhearing, there's been so much talk . . .

FATHER. I'm not accusing you of eavesdropping. I'm glad you know. You have a right to know . . .

(Sounds of war begin. The sons, who have been standing at attention and saluting all this time, run off the stage in fear.)

V

(The house is in shambles again. Their clothes are torn.)

FATHER. Well, say something!

MOTHER. All my ketchup, the aspirations of the children . . . And, for what?

FATHER. For me . . . When times were good nobody noticed the old man who supported them. No, there were songs and all manner of gay pursuits; midnight parties and garden romance, among the roses in scent under the moon; though the universe be vast, life is secure . . . But, should I stumble under the weight, should a child lie in the path of the projected series of my oxfords, whilst I, stumbling under the weight of financial burden, dazed, as it were, calculating, mind you, to avert the impediment, not only for the sentimental implication, but the danger implied therein of falling; not to mention the male neighbor, who must take this as a call to arms; and then the piteous choice of falling into his hands, or quickening my gait at the risk of injuring my heart . . .

MOTHER. But what has this to do with us?

FATHER. . . . Did anyone say, it's not Father's fault, that Father has become a victim of a crime that dates from the prime motion, owed to the Prime Mover . . . Through the billions of wombs man rose; cities like fungi growing out of campsites, came and decayed. New lands were discovered, the sword and the Cross, the fungus following its nutrition . . . We are premeditated, not by ourselves, but by the stars!

MOTHER. But man was useful; he had a need to craftsmanship, Father; even the rack and the gas chamber, they were made with an eye to craftsmanship, Father; even those to be killed dug neat graves for themselves; man was obedient to duty in spite of ill fortune . . .

FATHER. But they did seek a way out . . .

MOTHER. But in the end they knew the end had come.

FATHER. But they had to try, they might be mistaken; there might be a way out. It is possible to give up too early . . .

MOTHER. In that death will come no matter how we choose . . .

FATHER. But it can be kept off for a time . . .

MOTHER. Yet, no matter how we choose . . .

FATHER. But why should we go to meet it? If it is put off for five minutes . . .

MOTHER. But it comes, it squeezes five minutes into no time. Time is in continual decay, there is no avoiding the end . . .

FATHER. What are you talking about?

MOTHER. I've forgotten . . . Were we entering a truth . . . ?

FATHER. Well, I wish you would shut up and stop wasting what may well be the last part of my life and listening time with your babble.

MOTHER. What did I say?

FATHER. That's just it, nothing. Here I hoped to be led by philosophic steppage to suicide, that one escape route. But you are merely making noise disguised as philosophy. Have you no loyalty at all? Must I continually remind you that I am in grave danger emanating from the male neighbor, who has through the years sought some excuse to move against me . . . Now, in the time of crisis, at the apex of danger, in the midday of despair, in the deepest hole of wretchedness, when dreams of the garden, the roses in scent, moonlight and the mistress of the sexual quest . . . Ah, ah, all that was lovely, shuddering and breaking like an image on a lake; so the mind cracks and is made of disconnections . . .

MOTHER. But the children, not to mention the mortgage or the milkman's money, the money for the braces on Percival's teeth, and the special shoes for Oscar's flat feet, their uniforms, not to mention the insurance and the new lawnmower . . .

FATHER. There shall be a slight deferment of conveniences, to be sure. In time of hostility certain services will break down. No hope for it. Men are called away to service. We civilians manage until the boys come home; keeping the home fires burning, so to speak. Being most careful whilst tending the fires that we don't set the house afire; grave danger of inexperienced hands . . . Though setting the house afire, still, it is not forgotten that the very best of intentions lay at the root of the mischief . . . No no, we forgive you this time, but take care not to befoul the nest again . . . Promises, surely, magnificent oaths, worthy of documentation, the brave smile and the solemn handclasp . . .

MOTHER. Not to mention ketchup as a building block toward the new reachievement . . .

FATHER. Not to mention the garden, and the roses in scent, the moon at full, the werewolf at bay, and the loins at flood tide . . . Ah, ah, the woman described by moonlight and shadow . . . And, as I have said, the werewolf at bay, the dinosaurs long dead, yellow fever conquered, courtesy of the good Doctor Reed . . . Ah, ah . . .

MOTHER. And do not forget the ketchup . . .

FATHER. . . . Was it springtime? A light rain fell, and the essence of roses filled the air . . .

MOTHER. I was striking with the heel of my hand the bottom of the ketchup bottle . . .

FATHER. . . . The air fluttered with bird and blossom, and the wind in handsome deed blew clean the green wood, and it rose out of the spectral fogs like a ship out of a cloud bank . . .

MOTHER. Blop, out it came; blop . . .

FATHER. What?

MOTHER. The ketchup!

FOUR POEMS

LAWRENCE FERLINGHETTI

OVER THE RIVER

Note: In the summer of 1970 it was reported that Yevtushenko had plans to come to the USA and go down the Mississippi with John Updike on a boat. . . .

Passing over the Mississippi
                at thirty thousand feet
I see Yevtushenko down below
                   making like Tom Sawyer
                        floating down the river
                        trolling for catfish
When he gets to New Orleans
       the Russian consul
           will be waiting on the dock
              with a basket of hush-puppies
Kind of like the Commissar
         who took Voznesensky
            back to East Berlin
                 in his black car
                     after allowing him an hour
                        after our poetry reading
                           across the River
It is open season on poets
                 in international waters
And you can catch
           the very limit

IN A TIME OF REVOLUTION, FOR INSTANCE

I had just ordered a fishplate at the counter when
three very beautiful
fucked-up people entered
I don't know how or why I
thought they must be
fucked-up except
they were very beautiful
two men and one very
beautiful goldenhaired
young woman very
well groomed and
wearing sports clothes like
as if they must have
just gotten out of an
oldfashioned Stutz
roadster with top
down and tennis rackets and
the woman strode to the back
of the restaurant
found a vacant table and
strode back and
got the other two
beckoning with elegant
gestures and
the three of them
walked back slowly to the table
as if they were not afraid
of anything or anyone
in the place and
took possession of it with
lovely expressions and
the very lovely young lady
settled herself so easily
on the settee beside
the younger of the two men
both of whom had
lightbrown wavy hair not too long

and cut like Hollywood
tennis stars or anyway
like visitors from some other town more
elegant than ours and
they were obviously so much better
looking and so much better
brought up than anyone else
in the place
they looked like they might be
related to the Kennedys and
they obviously had no Indian or Italian
blood in them
and she obviously with
so many avenues open to her
with her two men
one of whom could have been
her brother
*I could not imagine her carrying
a carbine* and
she kept tossing her hair ever so gently out
of her eyes and
smiling at both of them and
at nothing in particular that I
could imagine and
her lips were moving gently with
her gentle smile and
I kept trying to imagine what
she could possibly be saying with
those perfect lips over
those perfect teeth so white
with her eyes now and then sliding
over and down the counter where
a lot of little people sat
quietly eating their quite ordinary
lunches while
the three beautiful people who
could have been anywhere
seemed just about to order
something special and

eat it with ice cream and cigarettes and
my fish finally arrived looking
not quite unfrozen and
quite plastic but
I decided to eat it anyway
She was a beautiful creature and I
felt like Charlie Chaplin eating his shoe
when her eyes slid over me
the Modern Jass Quartet
came over the Muzak speakers and
under other circumstances
in a time of revolution for instance
I *could* have fucked her

SHE OF THE SHINING EYES

She of the shining eyes
in the next booth
Ramada Inn Lawrence Kansas
Beautiful teeth and long hair
talking to a smiler in sharkskin
whose back I am faced with
She is twenty and aglow
saying something important
about their life together
It must be serious
the way she looks at him
with her far-eyed look
half-smiling
or maybe it is just about the tragedy
of some movie she's just been to
I can't hear the words
Just the voice lisping a little
flat almost
except for the eyes
He smiles into them

They are both smiling
into each other
Maybe it is just a little joke
between them
not a tragedy at all
There is nothing to do about it
in either case
Just watch it happen
amazed and aghast
at the fantastic craziness of it
and of existence
which just goes on
bowling us over
Set 'em up in the other alley
Wow watch this one
I got my crystal spectacles on
Soon soon their supper will come
Soon soon they will eat it
or each other
not necessarily a tragedy
She is giving him her
long look again
Soon the curious plastic-antique restaurant
will curl up around them
and blow away with them
over the plains of Kansas
not necessarily
an ecological tragedy
Maybe it is all just a goofy movie
about eating
He may be about to eat a fish
whose baked eye glares up at him
Soon soon they will devour each other
Eyes feasting on each other
each prepares the other's surrender
Soon she will look away
with her long look
out a window
through the Standard Station's neons

toward the plains
where somewhere soon
they will lie together hot
under the sun at noon
Soon soon she will finish eating
her appetizer
Soon soon she will look at him again
You can tell she's still hungry
Woman is a wonderful invention
of man
and he a strange seed in her
Soon soon they will be born again in the sun
Soon too soon they will be wonderfully done
with each other
It is the year 2000
and she is 2000 in a slurb
She looks away from him now
into the great American night
and seems to see very far
unless it's just contact lenses
making her eyes
so shiney
There is a great crowded bluff
in Lawrence Kansas
that looks a long way
into the astonished heart
of America

LETTER TO A YOUNG POET IN CUBA OR
MAYBE SPAIN

I have just discovered the Nineteen Sixties
in all the places and people I passed through
and all the trips I took
at the intersection of
the rotten cheese which is Europe
and the Bardo Thodol
in the intersection of
that European darkness not our darkness
and the First-and-last Frontier
which is San Francisco
in the intersection of
Hare Krishna and Kama Sutra
el orgasmo de dios
in the intersection of Quetzalcoatl and Fidel
Shiva and Allen Ginsberg
dancing in eternity
arms around each other
in the intersection of love
and of the Great White Whale stranded
between Charles Olson Jack London and Jack Kerouac
in the intersection of revolution & evolution
between too many turn-ons
and too many far-out trips
in the intersection of
two dreams and two deliriums
Drunken Boat and Sun Ra boat
hashish y bomba de hidrogeno
reino de politico de queso con mierda
I have just discovered the Nineteen Seventies
in the intersection of
the bad breath of modern poetry
and la voce del popolo
as the world sinks deeper & deeper
into the Kali Yuga
There's a high wind blowing
Watch out
when the shit hits the fan

Hummingbird Hummingbird die right on time
But the mind is still the sun
travelling through the sky
And the mind also rises
Abrazos revolucionarios
mis hermanos del Sur

TWO POEMS

ENRIQUE LIHN

Translated by William Witherup and Serge Echeverria

TRANSLATOR'S NOTE: *Enrique Lihn is a Chilean poet. He was born in 1929 in Santiago, and has published four books of poetry:* Nada se escurre *(1949),* Poemas de est tiempo y de otro *(1956),* La pieza oscura *(1963) and* Poesia de paso *(1966). The two poems that follow are taken from the last book, which won first prize for poetry from the Casa de las Americas in 1966.*

In the opinion of his fellow countryman, the poet Nicanor Parra, Lihn is the best of the younger Latin American poets writing today. One of the four judges of the 1966 Casa de las Americas competition, the Mexican critic José Emilio Pacheco, has this to say about Lihn's poetry:

"[The poems] . . . have little similarity with what is now being written in our language. Enrique Lihn . . . does not surrender himself to any trend derived from the great figures. The "lived space" of each man does not adjust to the words that others have conceived. . . . He seems to tell us between the lines . . . [that] ours has to be a critical period of examination and of use of our national and continental poetic heritage, incorporated into new situations and other necessities.

" . . . Lihn's poetry is characterized by its deep opening towards the real—fondness for realism is in the nature of his creative imagination. If he oversteps the limits of verse, his deft rhythm saves him from falling into shortened narrative or expositive

51

prose, and even the most immediate references, least susceptible to being converted into poetic material, are filled with meaning and lyric sense. In the silent course of memory incarnations follow recollections: lost childhood, cities, the sudden image of love, and they gain the general validity only accessible to a complete poet."

The Defeat *refers to the Chilean election of 1964, in which there were three candidates, a Socialist, a Christian Democrat and a Conservative. Prior to the national election, there was a municipal election in Santiago to replace a dead supervisor. The Socialist candidate received the backing of the Chilean Communist party and won by a landslide. In June, a deputy of the Communist party gave a speech in the House of Representatives in which he slandered the Chilean cardinal, archbishops, priests and so forth. This shocked many of the Catholics who might otherwise have voted Socialist. This incident and the election of the supervisor provided the anti-Socialist propaganda machine with new fuel. Should the Socialist candidate Salvador Allende win, they warned the mothers, their children would be sent to Cuba.*

The Chilean Communist party began to worry about the reaction. Perhaps the triumph of Allende might provoke a coup d'etat *sponsored by the United States and backed by Conservatives, which might bring about the end of Socialism in Chile. So the Party thought it would be better to let the Christian Democrats win and still keep Socialism alive as a legitimate opposition. The Christian Democrats did indeed win, and there were wild celebrations in the streets of Santiago.*

Lihn was sickened by all this and went into voluntary exile, traveling and living in Europe and Cuba. Allende's victory in the 1970 election, however, changes the perspective of the poem slightly, and perhaps Lihn will return to Chile. Still, The Defeat *remains more than a topical poem. It must be seen as part of that tradition of South American political poetry that begins in modern times with Ruben Darío and ripens with Pablo Neruda. And of Lihn's translated poems, it is certainly the most Brechtian.*

THE DEFEAT

Concentration of images, reveille of the real;
words restore power to the facts; and
                    the burning ghost of the new poetry
is an old man who closes his shop for the last time,
outside the walls of a city that has lost the memory
                    of its correspondences
with the boulevard Montparnasse,
the reason for dreams and the good sense of mystery.

It has been a long time, really, since I could
                    assist with the burial of the last of the first
                    of our magicians, but when I was very young
                    I knew his heirs.
That shadow, preserved from the impurities of usage,
                    was for some an excellent bone
                    wrapping—invisible armor, a commonplace
                    proof—for others,
                    the irony of a lighthouse
that lit up its own storms.
—And now, what do I do—said one of them; and it was not
                    a question, since he was almost fifty:
the author of some poems as dark as this desperate
night.

Reality has exposed us;
                    me to, especially, the distant nephew
                    of the stars that disappeared
by the magic art we can't practice anymore
                    without becoming guilty of the night;
vanished to the rhythm of fierce revolving gears in a
                    great necessary grinding
as if we errant spirits were superfluous.

Reality is what happens, and, in the center of it
                    and against it, the machine.
I don't regret it for anyone: to each one the torment of
                    his faltering steps, of his perversity or of his
                    insignificance.

Not even for me, perhaps, the last one to abandon this
             phantom ship because I was drunk
             the night before.
This is still an image. The first of those who
             preceded me in understanding that one
             can't be the last of them without running
             the risk of his luck.
Our enemies are too numerous to allow
             us the luxury of thinking about our
             friends.
Yesterday afternoon they passed her like a flooding
             river, the Jesuits having blown
             the dam;
in luxurious cars; in great floats
             and also on foot to encourage by their example
the ship's masthead of the poor in spirit. For
             these the kingdom of Heaven
and, in advance, the sacred horror of the communist
             hell, popular capitalism and its
             works of charity: bundles of old clothes;
therefore: a small share of existence
             under the old satraps.

    The machine, the machine.
It isn't one of those from the century's first decades:
             mutilation and ecstasy of the best spirits
nor this other one in which two parallel lines cut
             opposed by confabulated worlds.
with the same obsession to extend to other worlds.
    Would a moment of silence survive the war
             by the surprise of our dead
since, really, we are modest persons.
    It is a machine . . . I saw it the other day at
             the Paolozzi exhibition.
To these remote countries the undertow brings us only
             remains of structures distorted by distant
             explosions;
the sculptor proceeds with irony canceling the function
             of the forms and smelting into one piece
             airplane parts and various artifacts;

but we oscillate between inocence and
                ignorance and we couldn't make ourselves an
                idol of our machines but
                a machine of our idols.
What the hell: an undeveloped people,
involutions of usages and customs who sense
                adapts itself to the times
when prayer was the comfort of the whip
and the god of Spain the shame of the angels.
Our lost battles will have sewn
                fear in us;
our victories: the transfer of respect
from the heroes to those they followed in the order
                of rape
and the patriotic speeches.
        What does solemnly poor mean?
                The Century of the Lights
and our century of poor gas lights surprised us
                in shameful attitudes
organizing misery at the parish priest's, in
                the Great Back Yard,
in the struggle for primogeniture and against the
                Protestant dead.
Gentlemen of goatee and mustache, what an excess
                of honorable
statuary cut with the same scissors!
Many of them exactly like the others: the high collar
would save them from the scaffold.
We honor all kinds of tombs, even those
                we should blow to pieces.
Any family album hides the unscrupulous
                businessman beneath a lordly
                appearance, his hands gloved
after having plunged them into the Funds of Bribery.

        Chinemachinema. The mechanism is of an appalling
                simplicity for its manipulators, but,
                who among them
can establish order where the premeditated
                wickedness of chaos always reigned?

Form follows form and a vast deformity
                    moves the whole
heavily, in a fatal direction.

   I agree: the best engineers serve in all
                    the bands, only these exhausted their
                    talent
in presenting an old artifact under a new
                    appearance
sufficiently known and insufficiently
                    recognized
by the cheated victims of their plundering
                    who are taught to confuse
                    fatality with crime.
   Enough of farces!
It's known that they would use the techniques of the
                    miracle and where the planning of
                    the miracle is, the countries in which they operate
                    on a grand scale and those in which
                    partial operation is enough.
This refers to the hopes based
on the honeymoon with the resurrection of European
                    colonialism, beneath faces favorable to the New Deal.
   Who is to say no? Over this
                    point the parity of opinions and the
                    consensus of the steps in the drawing rooms
                    of the Palace.
Not even the most scrupulous skeptic would accept his
                    omission from the list of invited guests
to a reunion with the Good Old Days.
The ceremony is a national pastime: the parade under
                    the soft twilight
of the gala uniforms eaten by larvae.
To fresh air football and the evangelical Sunday:
                    sadness of another Garden of Olives in
                    which spirit and flesh ruminate, under the
                    same yoke, an agony covered with flies
                    on the dishes of grass.

But what can be expected from the barbarians.
Finally we have not replaced all our
                customs with theirs, a curious lack
                of concentration on the model
condemns our copies to a gilded mediocrity;
and, in any case, the rest of what we have
                agreed to call national dignity
                would be seriously slashed
                should they decide to adopt the air of our de-
                feat to add it to the celebration of the
                triumph, in this remote colony,
of the perpetuation of the cancer of their empire
in the alien guts.
A few hours ago (tonight and last night are
                confused; the triumphant noise of the
                silence of failure)
one of them, with a burning drunkenness,
was enjoying the street carnival on the
                carnival of the bus, a big dirty bastard,
fingers raised in a V for victory: the braids
                of a heavy Anglo-Saxon little girl who
                rode on a fierce stallion with an
                impassible pugnosed face.
The bulldog-man
spun around on his axis like clothes in
                the washer, elbowing the person
                next to him on the chest
                and shouting:
"I'm a North American. I'm a North American."
I wished his world would have sunk.
    It will be said: "an individual case" and the accusing finger
                must point to the impersonal factors
                that move the individuals
                the river where the fish go during their time
                to spawn;
"de la sociologie avant toute choses," but what a heap
                of obvious facts in those extreme cases
when clarity springs from the very pores of the
                corpus delecti
thrown quickly to the uncultivated land that the
                moon shows in front of the big housing projects.

It was enough to see that fellow to get
        a panoramic and well articulated vision,
        the unnecessary statistics in the last plans.
The difference between one Yankee and another
        represent, to us, a margin of
        unpredictable brutality in relation
        with the forces of an occupation said to be
        peaceful,
and a margin, also, for the cultivation of
        personal friendships in a No Man's Land.
The cultivation of friendship is a personal pastime, the
        entertainment of guests,
the moderation between Moors and Christians,
        the cessation of all antagonism
        at lunchtime.
In a small country loaded with traditions,
        formality before everything else, and the use
        of psychological violence
only in unusual cases.
The control, at a flagrant distance, of our old
        machine together with the promise of its
        restoration
in the hands of specialized technicians on the base of
        surplus and heavy industry.

    There is no doubt:
of the 60,000 FBI and CIA agents,
        only one or two have shown a thread
of their intent to climb the floats and
        occupy a swaying place
next to these beauties who eclipsed everything in the
        apotheosis of triumph, but the sense
        of our defeat.
It was all clear in spite of so much glitter and the
        brightness of the looks and the fireworks.

    The invisible army of occupation can fight
        while in bloodless retreat
and can afford to take up spring and summer quarters:
        fishing seasons in the southern lakes and
        harvest time in the metal deserts.

To the Pacific, to the Atlantic the battleships: here
                it isn't necessary to import peace
in the person of snipers and marines.
The iron belt may be loosened a little
on the other side of the Andes and tightened on the
                really strategic places
where the blood burns, bubbles and screams.

   It only seems possible to arouse a struggle
                between democrats and republicans far away from
        home
by using the Bomb on a small scale,
                razing the nurseries in the pastures
of the short, slant-eyed communists. A
                profound claw,
and then the parade of human rags in honor
                of Liberty and Democracy.

   This is what keeps strong men busy:
                "the struggle for Peace," one of them says to us
again occupying the panoramic stream
                that face as impenetrable as an expanding
                mushroom;
some iron crevices look at us, through it
                the real army is lost to sight
in its ascending march toward the abysses beyond
                the sky, striped with columns
                white with panic.
The eyelashes sewn where the lids fold are
                heaps of charcoal, and on the first blurred level
                nothing is known of what is going on
                in the other half of the hemisphere.

Military discipline suffers certain faults
                compensated according to the order
                of number and of strength.
Those boys don't march: they walk, each one
                "in the context of their personal liberty"
                —would say one of their myths—as if they
                could be directed by flaming clans in all
                directions.

To the cantina, to the bar, to the bowling alleys or to the
            human catacombs in the flaming
            stadiums.

    Under the closing eyes, the erosion in the
            bags of age: arid mountains filled
            with scars.
The message ends in what intends to be a
            call to wisdom but it is a total delirium
            that makes signs behind the threads
            of the Doric columns.
The orator thinks of death, and death, for the first time,
            of herself, with the
            perplexity of a prima donna
            suddenly raped by a horde
            of beasts, in her own home.
It is a death that allows the curious possibility of
            even killing herself
in a hydrogen bath.

    This discovery transfigures her: opulent beauty
            of Marilyn Monroe another St. Sebastian for
            the sexed hearts that would like
            to recover from the mutilations of the spirit
            in total butchery.
    But Man, The Fearless, The Hard One
only interprets "cleanly" of course to the
            majorities of his people that might
            turn against him, toward another.
No shadow of doubt has crossed that mask:
            the eagle flies high over the Appalachians,
between fifty stars homes of her pride:
the night filled with stars by the obsession of triumph.

    To be chosen by a chosen people
is not a task that can be accomplished exclusively
            on the level of human forces.
Absolute correctness in the addition of myths, such is
            the way of truth, the American Way,
            crossed by the Divines and the Saints
and those who sewed with their bones the time
            of the limitless drama of expansion.

To present a monolithic flank to the opponent, a
              carapace harder than a hundred of his,
              and under the cover veneered with irrational
              gilded symbols, the account book brought up
              to date:
in the Credit: the proconsul's jaw and the whistling
              of the whip on the sentry's boot, the
              multiplication of taxes and the
              sinking of the small provincial
              markets;
in the Debit: the bargaining with charity funds.
    For the exercise of a Manifest Destiny, the
              fatality is a wage in the office,
one would say the object of a special institutionalized cult
              in order to exorcise it.
Masochism is rampant in all of this:
Thanatos, the Blonde Beast's love of
              self-destruction, reduced to the gasping of
              the blonde Hottentot's struggle of all against all
              during which it has been progressively detached,
              from self-love together with big pieces
              of human substance
until it remained in the partiality of muscles
              and of bones.

    On the ballots the threat of the strongest will triumph,
the stabilization of violence under the face of Caesar,
              under penalty of falling in the inflation of the same,
              and in the dominion of small business
that will ruin the Empire's prestige.
It would be best to know it better than the opposition,
but it is still possible to respond to his blind harassment
              with a new Fourth of July speech.
An unparalleled greatness would be the appropriate leitmotif.
Without parallel: here is a good puzzle for the
              intellectuals disaffected from bread and circus, and
              who haven't succumbed to the voluntary poverty
              of the Venice of the West or to the
              drugs by the Ganges or in the caves
              of the Old World.
History could stop, the Tower of Babel reconstructed
              and the two-headed eagle flame in the sky.

THE GOOD OLD DAYS

And those of us who were sad, without knowing it, once,
            before all history: a divided people
—remotely close—among distinct childhoods.
Those of us who paid with hesitation for our forced
            permanence
in the garden when they closed the house for an hour,
            and received
the tortured remains of love under kind of
            a "holy patience"
or tenderness mixed
with a eucalyptus branch against unhealthy dreams.
"You are your poor mother's only support; you see
            how she sacrifices herself for all of you."
"Now go back and dream with the angels." Those of us
            who spent the superfluous summer
of poor relatives, in docility, under the
            perverse protective look
of the great uncle and lord; those of us who raised our faces
            to see him
giving the order to kill the sick beast with an ax,
            and then dozing
in his murderous sleep perfumed with peaches.
    Fragile, solitary, absent-minded: "I don't know
            what, doctor," but determined
to hide the hands in nocturnal fright, and
            associate ourselves with fear
through urine and to guilt through paternal punishment.
    Those of us who lived in the ignorance of older
            persons added to our own ignorance,
in their fear of night and sex nourished by
            an old bitterness
—remains of food that is thrown to sparrows—
            "You only remember the bad, I am not
            surprised:
it's an old family problem." But no,
            those of us who were
meticulously loved in the one and only possible
            sense of the word
that no one had said in fifty whole years,
            small engraved faces   seals of the alliance.

Yes, really the son of good will, of the
                    most hot and rigorous stoicism. But
                    isn't this a proof of love, the
                    acknowledgement
of the silent grief that envelops all of us?
    It is transmitted, close to the rocking chair and the
                    wall clock, this tendency to mutual
                    ignorance,
the habit of the cloister in which each one tries,
                    all alone, the same bitterness. Those
                    of us who promised ourselves
to reveal the secret of generation on our
                    birthday: a version limited to the doubt
                    over the flight of the stork and the loan
                    of obscure words surprised in the
                    kitchen, only to this
like giving away a package with medlars, or in the house
                    of the miser
the joy of the medicine given for dessert.
                    "Han-fun-tan-pater-han"
    Yes, the same curly copy according
                    to an ancient custom, riding, with gentle
                    seriousness, on the endless knees of the
                    paternal grandfather.
(And it is the time for remembering it. Grandfather,
        grandfather who
                    according to an ancient custom imposed
                    fearful respect among our children
with your single proud presence: the high boots and the
                    whiplash for the morning ride
                    under the poplars.
Boy from snow-covered lands that returned for you
                    in the secret of solitary old age
when the elders were now the others and you the man
                    who suddenly wept
since no one listened to him returning to his stories.)
                    "Han-fun-tan-pater-han"
    The same rider on old knees. "It's not
                    more than two years; then it was thought
that he was too sensitive a child."
The first to be surprised by our own
                    fits of rage or cruelty

this time, when the kitchen knife rubbed
    a sacred hand
or the other hand with which we neglected the red-hot coal
    on the floor,
        on the spot where we played barefoot;
flagrant victimizers of bottled butterflies:
death by iodine waters, crushing of the
        larvae on the grass and hunting
of the lizard in conspiracy with the author of
    death
by inflation in the bucket. Death by coupling
of big spiders in the glass cloister, and
    suddenly the violence
against the toys awaited all year long.
    "You need the patience of a saint."
  Those of us who had learned to sneak in on tip-toe
    to the maternal grandmother's drawing room; not to
    move too much, to keep respectfully quiet:
    supposedly bowing
to the memories of the Good Old Days offered to heaven
    without a mote of dust close to an examination
    of conscience and a tireless labor in the
    empty ant hole
and clean, clean, clean as the inside of a
    mirror that is wiped from within: each
    thing numbered, different, solitary.
The last ones called according to the ordering of time,
    but the first to reestablish eternity,
    "May God grant it,"
in the disorder of the world, nothing less than this;
    while we clipped and stuck
    colored papers:
stigma of St. Francis and hairs of St. Claire
    —barefooted people on snowy landscapes—,
and we were given a different gift each time:
    allegories of a Victorian love:
the typewriter and the Victrola. Those of us
    who were educated in this sort of love for the
    divine, in the weight of predestination and
    the cleanliness of nails;

respected and respectful guests at six years old;
> the confidents of a subtle anguish,
> their disciples in theology.
Ready, from the first moment, for baking
> in the oven, of faith poked by God
> and the devil, well mixed in flour
> to a perhaps excessive dose of yeast;
quickly inflated to the heat of catechism. Those
> who, instead of nocturnal pollutions,
> knew the ecstasy, the eagerness to attend
> Midnight Mass, the proselite eagerness
> of missionaries, the fear
of losing the dear ones to eternity,
> the vertigo of eternity grasped on the verge
> of the soul: an abyssmal cold, chronic
> and ineffable;
harmless remorse of conscience like the
> first toothaches: the incipient
> pleasures of self-torture
under a growing disguise, with wings down to the floor.

> In the future, the brevity of a Nietzche
> made of lard, cooked in itself;
> Weininger's transit chased by a
> soulless ghost. Now the slow revolving
> around crucifixion,
oppressed in the heart, Thinned in the blood,
> Heated in the breath.

YOU TOO CAN BE A FLOORWAX THAT EVEN YOUR HUSBAND COULD APPLY

DON WULFFSON

PART THE ONE

THE SUBJECT OF A NUMBER IS ORDINARILY ONLY AN-OTHER NUMBER.

OF HOW MANY SEXES HAVE YOU DENIED YOURSELF?

INDEED, HOW MANY SEXES ARE THERE? THREE? FOUR? perhaps each of us is an entirely unique sex, independent of all others; yet for each of us exists an opposite sex, man or woman.

ON THE OUTBREAK OF THE REVOLUTION OF FEBRUARY, 1848, MARX WAS BANISHED FROM BELGIUM. HE RE-TURNED TO PARIS, WHENCE, AFTER THE MARCH REVO-LUTION, HE WENT TO COLOGNE, GERMANY, WHERE NEUE RHEINISCHE ZEITUNG WAS PUBLISHED FROM JUNE 1, 1848 to MAY 19, 1849, WITH MARX AS EDITOR-IN-CHIEF.

STRATEGY
divide students into two groups. invite each to engage in creative enterprise. see who wins!

in the past we have viewed evolution as an historical phenomenon. it is important that we instead see evolution AS AN ONGOING ENLARGEMENT OF SELF.

I would try to pretend that nothing had happened. nothing is wrong my dear I would say, walking on my belly like a fish to the tree that grew in my room. get out of that tree she would say. I'm not in the tree I would say. I'm down here, in your hand.

IT MATTERS IF WE ARE WRONG!

I pulled a little deceit on her. it was tedious but pleasant. I wept a little. I rolled away from her. onto my stomach. I stuffed my face in the pillow. I grinned.

THE GREAT BOOKS, CONSUMPTION AND PRESUMPTION
it was a great surprise when I first noted that I presumed my students to be inferior to the materials they were expected to circulate.

suddenly there are reasons

IT MATTERS IF WE ARE WRONG
Are we oxidizing the minds of our children? Are we right in sending our children to schools?

I always try to hide my feelings—
They are suddenly too much for me,
When I turn and see my younger daughter

With tears running down her face.

HAD THERE EVER BEEN COLOR BEFORE THERE WERE
HOT DOGS
a caption outsiding a television commercial
                    wherein I love my lover I love
                    the grass   whereon her   feet   go

A TRAPPED OUTSIDER WHEREIN A NUMBER OF
ACTIONS HAVE A DISAPPOINTING TRACK SEASON
the dimension in which one may witness the progress of action must
of necessity be a slow dimension

THE OF COURSE NOT OF IT
electrical diagnosis is a thing of the past WHEREIN APPROACH-
NESS IS A GOING OUT OF NOT A CONSISTING OF

for example   tiger times   Plexus

the Rosy Crucifixion   the tree of life is kept

alive not by tears but the knowledge that freedom is real

and everlasting

THE SUM TOTAL OF ACTIVITY IS ACTIVITY
to survive stress must be on ACTIVITY AS OUTLET and AC-
TIVITY AS ENTERTAINMENT

later we could take a swim said the woman to her husband but the
evening gathers in shadows at my feet said the man to his wife

                    a THING WELL DONE IN THE PRESENT
                    IS a projection into the future OF A THING
                    NOT DONE BEFORE

(a man, for example, is held together only by the tension of his
thoughts)

TAKE FOR EXAMPLE MY FRIEND DOGGI
When approached this afternoon by the filling station attendant he
turned his mouth bashfully toward the car fill it up with what is
known as flite-fuel he said HE LOOKED IN THE WINDOW AT
ME AS THOUGH I SHOULD APOLOGIZE FOR HIM!

AUDITORY MISUNDERSTANDING
WE ARE MISTAKEN IN OUR CONSCIOUSNESS OF TIME
AS MATTER, AS SOMETHING AMENABLE TO REAL MA-
NIPULTION. IF THIS WERE SO, WOULD NOT SOUND
THEN CARRY OVER THE AGES?

Would we not still hear the ringing of the bells, and the chirping
of the birds, and the chattering of the voices of the past?

I was afraid to go swimming today afraid that once in the water
I would suddenly forget how to swim

it is an old fear and one that has haunted me all my days a
peculiarity of mind that has rendered me on more than one occasion unable to recall what I do for a living.

indeed I often pause when asked my name

I pause to rest

I stretch out naked upon my bed. My body turns to charcoal, then
to gray. Evening falls, and the wind blows into the room and cools
me.

The snail on the wall beside my bed has resumed a journey, begun
many days before, down my bedroom wall, leaving in its wake a
grand trail of dried crystals and snot. Last night I had thought it
dead, but this evening I find I have cause for rejoicing: the snail
is alive and has resumed its journey.

THOUGHT IS A GIMMICK WHEREIN THE THIRD LETTER
OF THE ALPHABET

WAS NOT ALWAYS C

AND

MAY NOT IN THE FUTURE BE C

COLD RECEPTORS VERSUS THE BOARD OF DIRECTORS:
return to Magic Mountain before it is too late. DIMINISHED
EXPERIENCE IS NO JOKE. IT MATTERS IF WE ARE
WRONG.

WANT TOO LITTLE AND DENY OVERMUCH? IT MATTERS
IF YOU ARE WRONG. WHATEVER DIMINISHES YOU IS
WRONG. return to Magic Mountain before it is too late. DIMIN-
ISHED EXPERIENCE IS NO JOKE. IT MATTERS IF WE ARE
WRONG.

I drink a cup of hot coffee, which runs out of me, down my leg.

everybody split! ice-cream cake is coming!
head for the bushes. its the best place.
noooo   not that way! the bushes.

bald men bald women bald children whole families of bald people
bald dogs the cat

I begin my letter once again dear me it begins oh dear me

I drink a cup of hot coffee, which runs out of me, down my leg.

I begin my letter once again dear me it begins oh dear me.

ANYONE FOR TENNIS?

From the beginning, Mary and Inez knew they would have to break, but how and when, and would either ever muster the necessary courage to precipitate the impending sorrow? Then again there was the question of Seigh T.

FUEL

Why did they keep a game going that long ago had ceased to be fun? How long could the ball be kept in play by two such indifferent players? Then there was the question of Gill T.

SHERRY T.

At one point there had been his growing sense of contempt and superiority. How imperceptible had been the change that left him resigned there to painless irritability and self-mockery. Then again there was the case of Sherry T.

THE CASE OF SHERRY T.

Originally there had been twelve to a packet, now there was only ten. Obviously there had been some hanky-panky going on. Who would make good for the missing two? Who but O. Transformer?

THE DECADENCE OF O. TRANSFORMER

In the first years of their marriage (it had been a second for both of them) she had been inclined to think of his three daughters as only numbers; there had been number one, number two, and number three. As the years went by she came to think of them as even less.

THE THREE DAUGHTERS

were sent away to college one by one as each came of age. The farewells were brief and formal.

SPAGHETTI AND WATER
In Cusco Sherry T. and Seigh T. said their good-byes, these has-
tened by the mutual attraction between Seigh T. and Gerald from
New York. (After all there had never been a greater bond between
them than the alliteration of their names.)

THE SUBJECT OF DRYDEN
The subject of their relationship was Dryden. A common interest in
the poet brought them closer together than close could, and more,
it helped each of them get past the first uneasy days of the relationship.

HOW FAST CAN YOU SLEEP?
Sherry T. fell asleep that night with the radio playing. (Perhaps it
was a need for some new companionship other than that she had
with Seigh T. that caused her to leave it playing.) In her dreams
she recalled her childhood, one scene in which she scrambled
through the underbrush with her father close behind.

JOHN'S NAME
John H_2O had all along been John Waterman. The transformation
of his name had ended with him calling himself John H. Or rather
it ended in Cusco with his death, given on the certificate as one
John Doe.

A DOG DOES NOT KNOW HIS NAME IS DOG
The success of the three youngest members of the family at the
university would have to be attributed not to intelligence so much
as to a habit of abasing themselves before any spectre of authority
encountered. And there were many.

FOR ONE THERE WAS HISTORY
Such a vast world for a young girl to get lost in!

YOU TOO CAN BE A FLOORWAX THAT
EVEN YOUR HUSBAND COULD APPLY

Inez felt that he was getting the short end of the stick (certainly this feeling was not new to him, for mixing with other people had in the past left him feeling inadequate). Once and for all his wife would have to go.

THE UNITED STATES OF COCA-COLA

All three girls complained bitterly of the social bruises they suffered at the university, though their Protestant upbringing encouraged them to suffer their privation like little Spartans. After all, said they, couldn't Seigh T. buy and sell the lot of them?

A CASE OF BUYING AND SELLING

Sherry T. realized she had a commodity to sell which, if advertised effectively, would bring her to the riches her father had taught her to expect, a fat checking account, a home in the right neighborhood, and a suitable make of automobile (a mere extension of her toe.)

UNCONTROLLED SALE OF DIAMONDS

q.v. the youngest felt it was experience that she lacked, and it was satisfaction that she wanted and satisfaction that she got.

(There is no introduction this time. Let me explain. I'm tired.)

(I got up this morning, angry as usual. Why the thought came to me I don't know, but anyway, I was thinking—"There will be no more introductions . . . and this will be the last.")

(This book has caused me enough heartbreak already. Let me explain. It began seven years ago in my head. It has not left me alone since. I cannot count the good times I have missed sitting at this typewriter.)

(Anyway, there will be no more introductions, not for a while anyhow.)

(I believe that a writer must communicate directly with his reader, and this I will do, whenever and wherever possible. Let me explain: My one desire is to entertain, and as an entertainer I want to make you feel you've gotten your money's worth.)

(This book is a revolution. If I am lucky you will find it hard to put down.)

(I had planned two forwards to this book; neither came to pass. I tried three times just to write the first—but that is another matter.)

(Perhaps all I have done here is satisfy my desire for a forward. Certainly this is no award-winning story—but that is another matter, so on with the Book.)

CAB FARE
(She knew she was in dutch with dad. She lay on her back. A Good Humor truck passed down the street. She put her hand in her dress and listened as the stupid, repetitious melody faded beyond the reach of her ears.

She awoke the next morning, still fully dressed. Seigh T. stood over her. She listened, but heard nothing. Apparently no one else was in the house.)

he who would declare the manifesto of the schools would ask that we explore new fantasies articulated since his youth WOULD HOLD THE HAND OF THE KINETIC MAID she who would remain seated where told HOW MUCH WE TEACH THROUGH FEAR how much better to teach through praise HOW MUCH WE TEACH OF THE PAST only the kinetic maid looks over her shoulder to see what is coming

BEWARE OF A TUNNEL WITH A MOUTH AT BOTH ENDS

for example   tiger times   Plexus

the Rosy Crucifixion   the tree of life is kept

alive not by tears but the knowledge that freedom is real

and everlasting

above all else you must REMEMBER the unity between falseness
and truth
     TRUTH AND FALSENESS OF UNITY
     THE BY DISTURBED BE NOT MUST YOU

THERE IS A HOLLYWOOD BOY WHO CALLS HIMSELF
JOHN AND BILL (He is a mystery.)

U AND EYE R A MR. E.   (You and I are a mystery.)

h
o
w
d
o
w
e
b
e
g
i
n
I
w
o
u
l
d
s
a
y
t
o
h
e
r
m
ybodyisinthegraveandithasturnedtosandanditmattersthatIwaswrong

FIVE POEMS

DAVID GIANNINI

By old geography the new bones grow,
As by old chrome the rich
Car dies; sky sights the eye in gold
Unknown, and the tiger
Homes in the lily.

The sillies keep correcting
The very serious conditions.
Repetition of the engines
Until so fast is slow.

Tiger homes in the lily,
Lily roars on the grass,
Inexactly and exactly as.

Sight, before the time of eyes occurs,
Before their time the eyes in eyes are
Seeing, seeing eyes inside: sighting.

An eye around the corner and
An eye rounding the corner
Meet, until completely: sight.

Around, ahead, the seeing time-
Wise tells: no time until
The time of eyes occurs, time occurs.

With the wreckage of my eyes

Occurs the simultaneous
Tumult of my thoughts which
Complete themselves when the
Breakage of my flesh recurs

On the broken mouth. This

Spoken aging is a forest
Arresting me, my life grown to
The depths of its greater wood:
The dead life of all my living

Becoming the insights of my dead.

There is a shadow without cast;
It has no place no time (no
Past), no one casts this shadow yet
It's cast. And this no-one's shadow
Is the man not seen because not born,
Not born because not seen, yet
How delicious and genius and madness!

Distance is invisible.
The invisible distance between
Us smoothes the unaccountable
Separateness of selves, soothes
My private world.

I receive you in my self and you take
Me.   Love.   And singleness
Interrupted.   Love that's given,
Love that's taken.   Love that's
Given, received, and broken
As the end of fire is coal, all
But the spark at the end:
Illimitable existence
Invisible in its distance.

FOUR POEMS

RICHARD MEYERS

FALLING ASLEEP

Falling asleep until I stop, far more tender
Than the sheets, with particles of sparkle
In me that must be in you
Too and I wish, knowing you
Love me most like this, that I could
Invent a phrase, a memory–
Capsule, a
Skin-soft capsule containing the creamy
Spell, which I drop in your coffee
To stop gravity
And signal you to see me almost alseep
When you're too far
Awake or too impatiently.

SUICIDE

Manmass, my breath like rope left
   Lying where I've been
I suck back. My thighbelly here,
   Eyes gathering
Every light, *knees breathe,* bloodrush
     In my back speaking sky: dead

Body, sharing molecules with bed–
   Clothes, mouth pulling
Milk from air, absolute secrets
   Shaft my brain like
Light through glass; in, *true,* In, Cock
     Rain Eye Globe. Strength went

Like semen till my body *fit* into
   The air. Dead: with
Senses wide as mirrors. beams to
   Every instance   But I
Can't sustain that utter solitude, shot
     with sugar through and through.

EQUATION

I have no knowledge of things
Taught me . . . I have no knowledge of
Not loving us. If I can only speak to or
See you with the tiniest spray
Of sex in the air mutually acknowledged, I
Like you in spite of anything.
That is, the most perfect version of
Love. *Despair*
Is a misperception of that
(Equation of my field
In walking down the street or sitting across
From you, at the farthest surface
Of which innumerable cocks barely touch
The cunts that grace your tactile aura)

ANATOMY

In my head is a three-armed barbell:
One end in my brain, two
Bulbs as substitutes for eyes.
The exterior of the barbell is
A gauze made of one-way-mirror strands,
And its interior consists of
The evening of May 9th.   The entire
Object is a phenomenon that for
Split seconds transforms the eyes
Into organs that register only cer-
Tain elements of events past, like
Suddenly realizing there was
Arsenic in that glass of milk.

At my chest is the siutation:
Scraped sky. My
Calves identify themselves as
"Caw." Meanwhile,
You may be under the influence of
A frantic butterfly attached by a long rod to
Your sense of delight. It's a complete mystery;
Our anatomy races
Threw out us at a rate
Through out us . . . *Suddenly*
I realize I'm *weightless—*
I
Assimilate the floor

INSCRIPTIONS

found in the fields of a new green city

BESMILR BRIGHAM

> *museum of the mind:*
>
> *we live in a room of antiquity*
>
> > *dug up bones*
> > *put together*
> >
> > *shattered char*
> > *from many a*
> > > *broken bowl*
> >
> > *the heart holds*
> >
> > *still to itself*
> > *irretrievable*
> > *an exterior (without*
> > *wonder*
> >
> > *walking through*

I THE ADORATION TOWER MASK

                                        spears
                            of the sun)

                            fall upon the altar

inside the crypt

the separated
leg bones
with the knee joint-hump
appear
extremely long—

half the height
of the spinal torso

below the chest
that lies . . .

decayed under coral—

a broken necklace
more durable than
bone

flat arms reach

lower than
the spread hips

and the hands
have fallen away from

circular coils of jade
and one false pearl

an idol
penis of stone
extends now
between the legs

and the skull
of harder shell

separates itself

an open conch
washed up
from that airless sea

                                     personage
                                     with 'joyas' of jade

                                     whose body shapes

                                     in hazard . . .

placed
in his mouth
the green stone

has eaten

deep to the heart

(a serpent-cross grows up out of the monstrous
figure of war
over the deserted hill (the mejoran

II JAGUAR

the death dogs
open their mouths
fiercely

the young king
sits on the throne
their joined bodies
make

one leg bends—
and his plain hands
motion time

yet not even dogs
could keep
                death away

though they
snarl
the king
rests on his own tomb
a whole race

                                    hurled
                                            and
                                    shattered
                                    and thrown into the bush

house of lions
that Waldeck copied
a century ago

only
fragments
are left

a portion of throne

a hand

              and one jaguar paw

III LA CRUZ FOLIADA: TREE CROSS OF PALENQUE

at the foot
of the steep steps
the dead king lay—
buried in rubble

           and guarded by
           six angels

a face
of stone
keeps his face—
holds in raised form
the life remembrance

the head
a death mask
of large cut mosaic jade
with conch shell
eye whites

about the iris
holes of fire

whose black centers
round their startled
obsidian . . .

struck in that dark
to watch the flesh go

and the flesh also

> of the six slaves
> buried as angels

(palace of exuberant joy

IV   THE ANGEL: FACE TURNED TOWARD US

> When he came up out of sea
> before the formed
>> civilization

> a man
nameless
Jorge or Jacobo
struggles with a monster

black infidel
looking out of stone

his arms
grip to the breast
and small legs of the animal
clutch
> pushing against
naked human form

its head
        a sea dragon
and the body with swirled
protective tail
resembles
a large ground lizard

                    or does it?
                    the conception lost

earth and sea—
bog garden of the wind
                        sold place
black chief
on twisted whip of his captive
with caught Jaguar eyes

stone circo, a pen
where the flesh devouring
    whose still coil holds the end of time—
surrounds the rock

lashed his crossed tongue to bleeding
shreds

and man—
conqueror of the dragon

                        look closely
                        to see if the thigh is marked

                        father of a race
                        struggling with his mind
                        concepts
                        against will of his body

before the mono the ape . . .
beating against wings of his angel

it is a picture
a child makes

from bone of the rock)

man

                    hunting down
with that
sea earth air animal
                    the woman
loins moved by the swan

making fire

                —to perpetuate himself

                    guerrero!

V   THE OFFERING STONE: OLMEC MONOLYTH

the figure stands
half lying on its long belly
as though a snake raised

older than the snake cult—
and is this
the meaning of . . .

                Queztal-coatl

                chained to the ground
                coiled in wing and feathers

a bare figure
lying on extended
body and tail—
with only the arms
and thrown-back head
human

arms
      appear first to be legs
curled legs of the earth dragon

the eaten-into rock at last shows their shape

elbows folded holding the front up
resting in length tight on either side
of the unmoving breast

      pulled at a strange angle
to center itself—
held up from the earth

in full form it makes an agony
look into the face!
the opened eyes
puffed full lips
            anthropoid
lower struck out
and slightly fallen

turned from concept with its pain
and supplication

rain pours
into the wide eye holes
water runs down
caught in the gaping mouth

and this bare globe head
human and animal!
forever
extends itself up
(arms like feet folded

        conscious misery
        'lucha postrema'
        first bitter Christ
        accepting . . . the cup

a round ball rolled upon the stone
bowl of suffering against the sky

the trumpet (urn

            'cara de mono al frente'
            baboon

            Ape man
            —whose god
            holds back the knife

            or he of light thrown from light
            who walked—
            and lay on his long hard belly
            cut down to the ground

            rolled in evil

            lifting himself up . . . a snake

VI   KABAL-CAHN

        with plumes for hair

        the day (a contingent god

        not to break the rock
        they hid him in a
                glyph

a face—

wounded on the wall
ad herido

nailed to the earth a live ram-stake

THE ISTANBUL PAPERS

WALTER ABISH

PART ONE

There's simply no room for a reappraisal. Yes, it's late in the day for such an undertaking. Disconsolately I sit at my desk at the Consulate thinking about Norman and Jack. But why, I persist in asking my fellow attachés, is everyone obsessed with winning . . . so carried away by the exhilaration of making a touchdown, and above all, so desirous of marching down the corridors of power . . . Listlessly I invalidate a few more passports after scrutinizing the most recent blacklist from the State Department. I've become increasingly convinced that little can be accomplished without a thorough understanding of Mao's writings. As usual, I spend the late afternoon rowing on the Bosphorus. What peace, what serenity. I let the boat drift, while I recline on the seat and gaze into the azure-blue sky. In my heart I embrace all mankind. I think back to my carefree days at Harvard . . . of the three of us, Norman, Jack and I . . . our convictions as yet untested, and our enthusiasm not the least bit blunted by the men who preceded us . . . who had gone through it all. We still lusted for the power and the fame that was rightfully to be ours. All of us unashamedly straining at the leash . . . ready to jump at the starter's whistle. How I must have let them down.

In all candor, I owe Norman and Jack more than I care to admit. I owe them my upright stance, my bravado, and my fearless pursuit of human dignity. Norman and Jack used to go out together on double dates, while I remained closeted in my room with the second part of *Epistolae Virorum Obscurorum* by von Hutten, who is not to be confused with the Baroness von Hutten zum Stolzenberg, who was born in Erie, Pa., some three hundred and fifty years ago. I always preferred inward communication, and also read medieval French texts. What did Norman and Jack ever see in me? I like to think it was my power of suggestion, as well as my hearty laugh. A hearty laugh, my mother used to say, cleanses the air of all suspicion. My eyes mist over.

PART TWO

Those inward dialogues, I keep telling myself, must discontinue. I try not to slack off at work. Now all attention is upon Cuba, and the newspapers carry in full Jack's latest response to the unexpected missile threat. Hardly any mention of Norman these days. Poor forsaken Norman. Like me, he must be quietly fretting away in some dank room. One day, mark my word, we will startle the world. In my own small way I have contributed to the phantasmagoria of our collective glory by being kidnapped for the third time, and consequently making all the local headlines. AMERICAN ATTACHÉ KIDNAPPED AGAIN, it said in bold Turkish print. This time I was away for three days . . . three long fly-infested days in an octagonal-shaped room with bars on the window. The Embassy was quite decent about the ranson. As soon as they shelled out the $375, I was set free. Just don't make a habit of it, said the Ambassador, when I thanked him for his intervention. The turbulent experience certainly adds new dimensions to my understanding of Man. I seldom go out now without a Smith and Wesson in my hip pocket. To my surprise the kidnappers displayed little interest in my friendship with Norman or Jack. I expect they thought I was exaggerating. Istanbul is a hive of intrigue. Unfortunately, the Embassy library leaves a lot to be desired. But there are so many other rewards. I am carried away by the slow emollient pace of the city . . . by the magnificent mosques with their sun-

basked courtyards . . . by the serene flow of the river, and by the
shiny eager faces of the young boys who beg for a livelihood.
Seldom has anything so succeeded in inspiring me. Tomorrow I'm
to meet Hitler's daughter. I have to thank Evans, the butler at the
British Embassy, for the introduction. He is rather too fond of
his Haig and Haig, otherwise we see eye to eye on almost everything else. There's to be no end to intrigue, I write my mother.
Hitler's daughter, indeed. I didn't even know he had a daughter.
How selective the eye can be, I brood as I watch a fly knock its
silly little head against the windowpane. Can flies see through
glass? My placid thoughts seek a release from the routine work I
do . . .

PART THREE

What a formidable woman, what intoxicating eyes. Over Turkish
pastries I chat with her about Rilke. The flawless Aryan profile is
enhanced by her shoulder-length blonde hair. At present she's
staying with two Turkish friends of Evans's. I do not examine this
delicate situation too closely. All the same there's much that needs
elucidating. How are your friends, Norman and Jack, she inquires.
I stare at Evans reproachfully, and he has the grace to look
ashamed. Can no one ever keep any confidences? We're hardly the
closest of friends, I explain to Otilla. We went to Harvard together.
You may have read accounts of our friendship in Esquire. Norman
was the chronicler of our youthful high jinks. He and Jack used
to go out on double dates. Sometimes they'd ask me to accompany
them, but my excessive passions compelled me to decline their
invitation. My explosive passions had to be kept in check. Were
you keeping yourself chaste, Otilla asks with a look of amusement.
The word "chaste" does not sit well with me . . . but an unforeseen
attack of abdominal cramps saves me from making an utter fool of
myself. After all, why quibble over a word? Mao did not quibble
when he undertook the Long March . . . or the broad swim. When
I return from the bathroom I find that Evans and his two friends
have left. Otilla speaks wistfully of the United States. It is a
society where so much can transpire. You can say that again, I
exclaim. She looks at me inquiringly, and then forthwith, in all

innocence, obligingly repeats the remark. The poor dear. She too
has many sad memories. One cannot help but be affected by them.
Certainly, her days were not all butter and roses at the Wolf-
schantze. We sip coffee on a low divan . . . and hold hands. How
serene the Bosphorus, and the slow gait of the throngs in the
crowded streets of this resplendent city with its cupolas gleaming
in the mercurial light of the late afternoon. I leave her side in the
early hours of the morning. What will all my Jewish friends think
of me? I can barely control my urge to sing in the shower after
I get home at 5 A.M. My jubilation is firmly rooted in love. I've
always known that one day I should meet a woman who would
deserve my respect.

PART FOUR

Evans is nursing his fourth Haig and Haig. He has come over for a
game of slapjack. To think that I've always stood in awe of English
butlers. They are, I still believe, Britain's principal monument—its
answer to Angkor Wat. Evans is no exception to the rule. His rigor-
ous training has been of inestimable help to him as he forms snap
judgments of each new international crisis. Otilla's falling for you,
old chap, he cheerfully declares. If only she was someone else . . .
if only Norman didn't feel such a passionate dislike of all Germans.
After all, what is past is past. I keep urging her to write her
memoirs, but she's only interested in cooking, said Evans as he
pocketed his winnings. Before taking his leave he asks me if I
happen to know any American publishers. Only the ones whose
passports I have stamped, I reply stiffly. You realize, don't you,
that we have an enormous responsibility towards her. Why, her
recollections alone might drastically change the prevailing view
of the Third Reich. But you just said that she doesn't want to write,
I point out to Evans. Barely controlling his irritation, he coldly
replies that that has never prevented anyone from being published.
That night I dash off a short note to Norman. Hitler's daughter
alive and well in Istanbul. I think I may be falling in love. Desperately need advice. P.S. Who is your present publisher?

PART FIVE

Receive back a stormy letter from Norman sent by special delivery. He threatens to publish it in *Partisan Review* unless I straightway submit it to *Commentary*. Hitler's daughter hasn't gone over too well with him. Some people can't seem to rid themselves of all that old film footage of World War II. It's that eye for an eye all over again. The remainder of the letter is devoted to Cuba. Norman insists that Jack intends to bomb downtown Havana. At times he can be laughably childish. Bomb Havana! What next? I spend the afternoon with Otilla, rowing on the Bosphorus. She loves American cooking, and speaks reverently of pumpkin pie and chicken-in-the-basket. Her mother, a von Huttenau zum Kastanien-vogel (no relation, of course, to Ulrich von Hutten, 1488–1523, author of the second part of my beloved *Epistolae Virorum Obscu-rorum*) had met Hitler at a vine festival in Salzburg. According to Otilla, it was love at first sight. At night I feverishly type twenty closely spaced pages about Hitler's favorite dishes. Evans introduces the only sour note by harping on my failure to stamp a visitor's visa into Otilla's passport. It could wreck my career. I prefer to follow the proper channels. He jeers at that. Don't you want to show them up, he asks, and stride shoulder to shoulder with Norman and Jack down the corridors of power? He's been reading too many novels by C.P. Snow, but he has also placed his finger on my Achilles' heel. My face turns white. I too think of the royalties her memoirs would bring. Enthusiastically I agree with Evans that she deserves a fresh start. I dash off another letter to Norman. I'm thinking of marrying Hitler's daughter. Please advise . . .

PART SIX

When together with Otilla I try to skirt the dangerous reefs of the past. The less said about papa, the better. I look deep into her stormy eyes, and see the tall fir tree forests of her Bavarian child-hood. I detect Till Eulenspiegel in her dreamy smile. Oh, how I look forward to the merry pranks after lights out. I speak privately to the Ambassador's secretary, a hefty girl from Milwaukee. But

she's appalled at the revelation of Otilla in Istanbul. Stay clear of
her, she warns me. We don't want the wires from the White House
to start humming. In the meantime Evans is becoming increasingly
worried. The visitor's visa is not forthcoming, for which, according
to him, only I am to blame. Things reach a head when Evans
threatens me with my own unloaded Smith and Wesson. I laugh
in his face. Go on, I taunt him. Pull the trigger damn you. We are
both equally taken aback when he obligingly does so. After hearing
the dry click of the unloaded weapon, Evans uncharacteristically
breaks down and sobs. It is most embarrassing. Of course I forgive
him. Early the next morning I receive a telegram from Norman
requesting additional information. What is she like? Send photograph. I love Amerika with all my soul, Otilla confides to me.
Slowly, hand in hand, an immense cavalcade of men and determined women proceed to climb to the pinnacle. Will I ever reach
it, I ask Otilla. What is the view like from up there? The local
newspapers are still full of talk about Cuba. Apparently it's to unleash or not to unleash the Air Force, that's preoccupying Jack.
Will he select Norman as an eventual go-between, I wonder.
Norman's heart, Jack always used to say, is in the right place. I
know where Norman's heart is, I used to reply. It's his magnetic
left hook that I'm worried about. But Jack would never hear any
criticism of Norman in those sun-kissed days at Harvard. He was
that sort of a person . . . upward bound, self-confident, heading for
the center of the storm and the Presidency. I doubt if he ever
chuckled over Diderot. Diderot could wait as far as he was concerned. In the final analysis my mother was right. Don't drift into
corners, she said. Keep mingling . . . no one ever disdains a happy
heart. If only I had payed attention to her advice. I often think
of those hectic days, standing shoulder to shoulder with Norman
and Jack in the quadrangle. Only their dreams have come true.

Of late I am surrounded by deep pockets of silence at the Consulate. Has word leaked out, I wonder. You and your big mouth,
grumbles Evans. But he has not given up hope of persuading me
to stamp Otilla's passport. I tell him that I need more time to think
about it.

PART SEVEN

Will you take me to Amerika, she whispers, after I rapturously
embrace her, and rain kisses on her unprotesting mouth. The
presence of Evans and his Turkish friends with this unexpected
display of passion . . . quite the contrary, I find that it inspires
me to fresh peaks of love and desire. I breathe in her Teutonic
perfume. I can almost discern the rattle of drums in the background. Hitler Jugend be damned. If Jack can profess to be a
Berliner, I don't see why I can't be the lover of Hitler's daughter.
Will you marry me, I ask her. Upon our arrival in Amerika, she
replies unhesitatingly. Women have always been able to twist me
around their little fingers . . . their jewel-studded, adorable little
fingers. Norman calls me unstable in his latest letter. Look who's
talking. Norman is quite a pacesetter in instability himself. Otilla
returns my volume of Diderot, *Jacques le fataliste et son maître.*
There's a large butter stain on the dust jacket. I have only myself
to blame for not protecting it with another paper. Otilla doesn't
even once refer to the stain, something I find mildly disconcerting.
I must admit that I now have second thoughts about our hasty
engagement. What will my mother think . . . and Norman, and
Jack . . . not to mention the State Department. But I keep telling
myself that I mustn't be too harsh on Otilla. God knows what life
must have been like in those bleak days of '43 and '44, surrounded
by imbeciles like Goebbels and Goering. Without much success,
I urge her to move into another apartment. Shyly she slips her
passport into my pocket. I breathe a sigh of relief when I open it
later and see that she uses her mother's maiden name, von Huttenau
zum Kastanienvogel. All the same, I spend a sleepless night tossing
in my narrow bed. The next morning I take matters in my hand
and apply for a leave of absence. To my surprise it is granted immediately, no questions asked. I have come to recognize that one
of my chief drawbacks is my failure to communicate the intensity
of my feelings.

PART EIGHT

Evans, his two cronies and myself see Otilla off on an Air France
jet. My worries are just beginning. I can get fifteen years for what
I've done. Even with a few years off for good behavior, it'll take

me out of the race forever. Norman promises to meet Otilla at the
airport. No snappy Nazi salutes, please! I caution him in my last
letter. I spend the next day straightening out my desk at the
Consulate . . . shake hands all around, and take off for a few days
with mother. Norman informs me, when I speak on the phone,
that Otilla is staying in a furnished room in Brooklyn Heights.
How would you like Hitler's daughter as a daughter-in-law, I ask
my mother. She falls down in a dead faint, causing me no end of
concern. Where is my heart, I keep asking myself while anxiously
gazing at myself in the mirror. This has to stop. Four days later I
fly to Washington. To my dismay Jack is curt when I ring the
White House. No invitation to lunch. All the same he invites me
over, and we have a long chat in the oval Blue Room. The respon-
sibilities of the office he now holds has dampened much of his
former enthusiasm. He seems less receptive, and hardly pays any
attention to what I have to say about Turkey. Past friendships, I
have come sadly to realize, soon turn into liabilities. Poor daunt-
less Jack, too loyal to discard the memories of our somersaults and
headstands at the Harvard gym. Dutifully I put him into the
picture about extending visitors visas for tourists from Turkey.
When I mention Norman, Jack frowns. To think that I once considered him to be a friend, he declares angrily.

You mustn't take everything he says to heart . . . I mean, where
would we be if we did . . . we'd be white Negroes, ha-ha. But Jack
doesn't join in the laughter. If you must know, after Castro, Norman is my most vexing problem. I know better than to ask Jack to
explain. You don't become President by explaining what you mean
every time you open your mouth. I leave the White House, still
musing over his last remark.

PART NINE

The following afternoon I visit Norman in his luxurious pad. He at
once offers me a drink, after which we compare our lifelines, and
wrestle on a Japanese mat. As usual he wins. I wish he wasn't so
bloody infantile. I particularly resent Norman's smug look after he
wins a wrestling match. When I mention having seen Jack the day
before, Norman crows triumphantly. I beat him, he shouts. Always
this insistence on beating people. It gets me down. I attempt to
compose myself while he explains that he had threatened to turn

all my letters to him, written on the Consulate stationary, over to the press the moment Jack ordered the bombing of downtown Havana. Former college friend of the President in love with Hitler's daughter now in Istanbul, would have made front-page news. You ruined my career, I howl. Go publish it in *Partisan Review,* he says peevishly, and refuses to give me Otilla's address. I leave with a heavy heart, nursing the ugly bruise on my chin where he hit me. Otilla, where are you? I place a number of ads in the personal columns of the *Village Voice.* I would never have suspected that so many women were named Otilla. Alas, none of the letters I receive are written in the spidery Gothic hand I have come to love.

Evans, forever an optimist, keeps sending me, care of my mother in Wisconsin who then forwards them to New York, sheaves of paper with Otilla's purported autobiography. Such lies, such fantastic lies. He wants me to edit it and get Otilla to sign every page. Nothing I say will convince Evans that I can't locate Otilla. Norman gave Jack his word that if Havana remained unscathed there would be no scandal. But why, why, why, I keep asking myself as I gently bang my head against the bathroom wall. I have served my purpose, I suppose. I still find it difficult to believe that Jack would give in to Norman's threat . . . I have always maintained behind Norman's back that he, Norman, was a massive windbag. All the same, not one bomb was dropped over Havana. With Otilla in his hand, God knows what Norman may next contemplate doing. I have not given up my search for Otilla. Once I thought I saw her leaving Schrafft's. I really don't think it was love after all. Yet I'm still upset by Norman's novel. All that talk about double dating with Jack at Harvard . . . and my heart almost burst when I reached the part of dealing with the German maid. Norman, have you no sense of shame. The sheer perversity took my breath away. Worse yet, he is the sort of person who would practice what he preaches. I called my mother in Wisconsin to tell her about it. Will I ever reach the mountaintop? What is the view like from up there? But there's lots of time. I am being posted to Beirut next month. The Istanbul Papers sent me by Evans, as well as the twenty pages I typed about Hitler's preference for chopped liver, are under lock and key at my mother's house. She is keeping her fingers crossed that no one will kidnap me in Beirut. I wonder, will I bump into Norman when I finally reach the pinnacle?

MARITIME ODE

ÁLVARO DE CAMPOS (Fernando Pessoa)

Translated by Edwin Honig

TRANSLATOR'S NOTE: Fernando Pessoa, Portugal's greatest poet since Camoës, was born on June 13, 1888, in Lisbon, and died there on November 30, 1935, practically unknown and unpublished. His poetic works were divided among four heteronyms, or personae: Ricardo Reis, a classicist poet, Alberto Caeiro, a primitive sage and antipoet, Alvaro de Campos, a futurist, and Pessoa himself, writing in both Portuguese and English. ("Twelve Poems" by Caeiro, translated by the late Thomas Merton, appeared in New Directions 19.)

"Maritime Ode" was first published in the second (and final) issue of the avant-garde *magazine* Orpheu, *in June of 1915. The author, Álvaro de Campos, as imaginary as his literary master, Alberto Caeiro, but also as real as his creator, Fernando Pessoa, is a neurotic disciple of Marinetti and Whitman. A marine engineer trained in Glasgow, de Campos lives in semiretirement in Lisbon and has no idea what or whom to believe in, completely cut off from the past as well as the present.*

Alone, on the deserted dock, this Summer morning,
I look out along the sandbar, I look out toward the Indefinite,
I look, and I am happy to see,
Small, black, and clear, a steamer approaching.

It appears so neat and classical by itself, so far away.
It leaves on the air, far behind, an empty banner of smoke.
It comes in, and the morning comes with it, and on the river
Here and there, in keeping with maritime life,
Sails are hoisted, tugboats advance,
Small boats hover behind vessels tied up at the dock.
A vague breeze rises.
But my soul belongs least with what I see,
With the approaching steamer,
Because it belongs with Distance, and with the Morning,
With the seagoing sense of this Moment,
With the sad sweetness rising in me like nausea,
Like the beginning of wanting to vomit, but spiritually. . .

I look at the far-off steamer with a great independence
          of spirit,
And in me a flywheel begins to whir, lightly.

The steamers coming in along the sandbar in the morning
Bring with them, in my view,
The sad and happy mystery of arrivals and departures,
Bring memories of far-off docks and other moments,
Of other customs of common humanity in other places.
All the hauling in and all the sailing off of ships,
And—this I feel stirring in me as if it were my own blood—
Unconsciously symbolic, terribly portentous
With metaphysical implications
That painfully dredge up in me the man I once was. . .

Ah, the whole dock is a nostalgia of stone!
And when the ship by the dock starts to put out to sea
And then suddenly stops so that a space opens up
Between the dock and the ship,
A new dread—I don't know why—comes over me
With its mist of depressing thoughts
Glowing in the sunlight of my cropped anxieties
Like the first windowpane hit by the rising dawn,
And I am swaddled, as with the memory of some other person
That mysteriously becomes my own.

Ah, who knows, who knows,
If once, way back, before becoming myself,
I did not leave from some such dock; if I, a ship
In the sun's slanting dawn light,
Did not depart from some other port?
Who knows if I did not leave behind,
Before this hour of the external world I see
Raying out around me,
A big dock lined with a thin crowd of people,
In a large half-awakened city,
A big mushrooming, commercial, apoplectic city,
Much as this one might be, out of Space and out of Time?

Yes, from a dock, from some sort of substantialized dock,
Real and made visible as a dock, actually a dock,
The Absolute Dock from whose unconsciously imitated pattern,
Unknowingly evoked,
We men build
Our real stone docks over real water,
Which after they're built are suddenly called
Real Things, Spirit Things, Entities in Stone Souls,
In certain moments of root feeling,
When in the outer world, as if a door were opened,
And, without anything having changed,
Everything becomes different.

Ah, the Great Dock from which we depart in Nation Ships!
The Great Original Dock, eternal and divine!
From what port? In what waters? And how is it I dream
        of this?
The Great Dock like other docks, but the One and Only Dock.
Like them full of the rumbling, predawn silences
Blossoming into morning with the grinding of cranes
And the arrival of freight trains
Under the occasional light black cloud
From the bowels of nearby factory chimneys
That hides the black floor of glinting coal dust
Like a cloud shadow passing over dark water.

Ah, what essence of mystery and meaning lies suspended
In the divinely revealing ecstasy
Of hours colored with silence and anxieties,
And which is no bridge from any dock to the Dock!

A dock darkly reflected in motionless waters,
The bustle on board ship,
Oh, the roving, restless soul of the boarding passengers,
The symbolic milling crowd among whom nothing abides,
And among whom, when the ship returns to port,
Some change has always occurred on board.

Oh, the continual flights and departures, drunk
      with Diversity,
The eternal soul of navigators and their navigations!
The hulls slowly flashing in water
As the ship takes off from port!
To float like the core of all life, to break like a voice,
To live the moment tremulously on eternal waters,
To wake up to days more direct than any in Europe,
To see mysterious ports on the wide wastes of the sea,
To round distant capes and come upon sudden vast landscapes
Past countless astonished palisades. . .

Ah, the remote beaches, the docks caught from far-off,
And then the beaches looming up, the docks seen from close-up.
The mystery of every departure and every arrival.
The sad instability, the incomprehensibility
Of this impossible universe
Felt at every maritime moment in its own skin!
The preposterous catch in the throat we feel to the core
Over the expanses of various seas with isles in the distance,
Over the far-off island coasts left behind as we pass,
Over the ports growing clearer with houses and people
As the ship approaches.

Ah, the morning freshness of one's arrivals
And the morning pallor of one's departures,
When the bowels tighten
And a vague sensation like fear
—The ancestral fear of moving off and leaving,
The mysterious ancestral dread of Arrival and Newness—
Shivers our hide and torments us,
And the whole of our anxious body feels,
As if it were our soul,
An inexplicable urge to be able to feel this in some other way:
Nostalgia for anything whatever—
A confused tenderness for what vague homeland?
What seacoast? what ship? what dock?
But the thought sickens us,
Leaving only a great emptiness inside us,
A hollow satiety of maritime moments
And a vague anxiety that could be tedium or sorrow
If only one knew it. . .

The Summer morning is still a bit cool,
The soft torpor of night still moves in the upcoming breeze.
The flywheel inside me moves faster, lightly,
And the steamer begins to come in, as it undoubtedly must,
And not because I see it move in from its excessive distance.

My imagination has it already nearby and visible
Through the full length of its row of portholes,
And everything about me starts trembling, all my body
          and all my skin,
Because of that person who never arrives on any boat
And whom some oblique message tells me to expect today
          on the dock.

The ships that come in by the sandbar,
The ships that leave from the ports,
The ships that pass in the distance
(I seem to see them from a deserted beach)—
All these ships in their almost abstract passage,
All these ships move me as if they were something else.
And not simply ships coming and going.

And the ships seen from up close, even when one doesn't
        board them,
Seen from below and from rowboats, with high iron sides,
Seen inside, through the staterooms, dining rooms, holds,
Seeing the masts from up close, pointing way up,
Leaping through cordage, stepping down clumsy gangways,
Smelling the oily, metallic sea mixture of it all—
The ships seen close by are something else and the same,
Stirring the same nostalgia and the same hankering
        for something else.

All seafaring life! Anything to do with seafaring life!
All that fine seductiveness of the sea enters my blood
And I dream indeterminately of voyages.
Ah, the far-away coastlines, flattened on the horizon!
Ah, the capes, the islands, the sandy beaches!
The oceanic solitudes, like certain moments on the Pacific
When, I do not know by what suggestion picked up at school,
One feels dragging at one's nerves the fact that this is
        the biggest ocean
And the whole world and the taste of everything becomes
        a wasteland inside us!
The more human, more splattered expanse of the Atlantic!
The Indian, most mysterious ocean of all!
The sweet Mediterranean, with nothing mysterious about it,
        oh classical sea dashing
Up the esplanades seen by white statues from nearby gardens!
All seas, all straits, all bays, all gulfs—
I'd like to clutch them to my breast, feel them in my arms,
        and die!

And all you seafaring things, my old dream playthings,
Compose beyond me my inner life!
Keels, masts, and sails, helm wheels, ropes,
The funnels of steamers, propellers, topsails, pennants,
Tiller ropes, hatchways, boilers, engine-sumps, valves—
Fall through me in a heap, in a mountain,
Like the mixed contents of a locker littered on the floor!
Be the hoard of my febrile avarice,
Be the fruits of the tree of my imagination,
The theme of my songs, the blood of my veined intelligence,
Let yours be the thread of esthetics that binds me
            to external things,
Give me metaphors, images, literature,
Because in actual fact, seriously, literally,
My sensations are a ship with its keel in the wind;
My imagination a half-sunken anchor,
My anxiety a broken oar,
And the weave of my nerves a net to dry on a beach!

Just by chance, a whistle sounds off the river—only one.
Now the base of my whole psychic system is trembling.
The flywheel inside me whirs faster and faster.

Ah, the steamers, the voyages off to I don't know what places
Of old So-and-So, the sailor, our old friend!
Ah, the glory of knowing that a man who used to walk here
            beside me
Was drowned off an island in the Pacific!
We who go on walking as he did will now discuss it
            with everyone,
With legitimate pride, an impalpable conviction
That all this has a finer, a vaster meaning
Than even the loss of the ship where he went down,
Went down to the bottom because water got into his lungs!

Ah, the steamers, the merchant ships, the schooners!
The sailing ships—alas!—becoming rarer on the high seas!

And I, who love modern civilization, I who embrace the machine
    with all my heart,
I, the engineer, the civilized mind, the man educated abroad,
I would like to see nothing before me but schooners
    and ships built of timber,
And hear of no other maritime life than the old seafaring life!
Because the ancient seas are Absolute Distance,
Pure Extension, free of the weight of Actuality. . .
Ah, how everything here reminds me of that better life,
Of those seas that were vaster because sailed more slowly,
Of those seas more mysterious because so little was known
    about them.

From far-off each steamer is a sailing ship nearby,
Each ship seen from afar now, is a ship seen up close
    in the past.
All the invisible sailors aboard ships on the horizon
Are the visible sailors back in the time of sailing ships,
Back in the slow-moving sailing age of dangerous voyages,
Back in the age of canvas and timbers and of voyages
    that took months.

Little by little the spell of seagoing things comes over me.
The dock and its ambience penetrate me physically,
The tide of the Tagus floods all my senses
And I start dreaming, I start wrapping myself up in a dream
    of waters,
Driving-belts start winding themselves firmly around my soul,
And the fast-whirring flywheel clearly shakes me.

Waters are calling me.
Seas are calling me.
All distances raise a bodily voice and call me,
And all maritime ages known in the past are calling me.

It was you, Jim Barnes, my friend, the English sailor,
    it was you
Who taught me that ageless English shout,
Which for such complex souls as mine
So venomously sums up
The confused cry of the waters,
The implicit, unrecordable voice of everything at sea,
The shipwrecks, the endless voyages, the hazardous crossings.
That English shout of yours, universalized in my blood,
Like no other shout, without human form or voice,
That tremendous cry that seems to resound
Inside a cave whose vault is the sky
And telling of all the sinister things
That might occur Out There, in the Sea, at Night. . .
(You always pretended it was a schooner you were calling,
And as you said it, cupping a hand at either side
      of your mouth,
Making a megaphone out of your big dark tawny hands:

Ahó-ó-ó-ó-ó-ó-ó-ó-ó——yyyy. . .
Schooner ahó-ó-ó-ó-ó-ó-ó-ó-ó-ó-ó-ó-ó-ó——yyyy. . .)

I listen to you, here and now, and am alert to everything.
The wind trembles. The morning rises. The heat begins.
I feel my cheeks redden.
My conscious eyes dilate.
An ecstasy rises in me, spreads, goes forth,
And with a blind upsurge of feeling the living flywheel
In me keeps time with it.

Oh clamorous outcry,
Your heat and fury bring boiling up inside me
All my fears in one explosive unity,
All my boredom turns dynamic, every bit of it! . . .
A cry hurled at my blood
From some past love, out of where I do not know,
But coming back and still with power to attract
      and to repel me,
Still with power to make me hate this life
I spend of physical and psychic impenetrability
Among the real people I live with!

Ah, just to get away, I don't care how or where!
Just to take to the high seas, through perilous waves and oceans,
To be off toward the Far Away, to Outer Space,
        to Abstract Distance,
Indefinitely, through deep mysterious nights,
Carried like dust by winds, by gales!
Moving, moving, moving, again and again!

All my blood rages for wings!
My whole body shoots on ahead!
My imagination rushes out through torrents,
I trample over myself, roaring, throwing myself
        down into it! . . .
My anxieties explode in foam
Where my flesh is a wave setting out to break against rocks!

As I think of this—o madness!—as I think of this, o fury!
Thinking of my straight-and-narrow life,
        full of feverish desires,
Suddenly, tremulously, extraorbitally,
With one viciously vast and violent twist
Of the living flywheel of my imagination,
Those breaks through me, whistling, trilling and whirling,
This somber, sadistic envy of all strident seafaring life.

Hey there, sailors, topsmen! Hey, crewmen, pilots!
Navigators, mariners, seamen, adventurers!
Hey, ships' captains! Men at the helm and the masts!
Men asleep in their crude bunks!
Men sleeping with Danger and keeping the watches!
Men sleeping with Death for a whole crossing!
Men standing on decks, standing on bridges looking out on
The immense immensity of the immense ocean!
Hey there, you winch-crane operators!
You furlers of sail, stokers and stewards!

Men who load cargo in the holds!
Men who coil ropes on deck!
Men who wash down the hatchways!
Men at the helm, men at the machines, men at the masts!
Hey there, hey there, hey there!
Men in peaked caps! Men in mesh undershirts!
Men with anchors and crossed pennants decorating their chests!
Tattooed men! Men with pipes!
Men darkened by so much sun, blasted by so much rain,
Made sharp-eyed by so much immensity before them,
Tough-looking because of all the winds they stood up to!

Hey there, hey there, hey!
Men who saw Patagonia!
Men who shipped out to Australia!
Men whose eyes filled with shores I'll never see!
Who made for land in places where I'll never set foot!
Who bought crude goods from the natives
          in the hinterland stations!
And who did it all as though it were a matter of course,
As though it were all natural,
As though that's what life was like,
As though they weren't even fulfilling a destiny!
Hey, hey, hey, hey, hey, hey!
Men of the modern seas, men of the ancient seas!
Pursers! Galley slaves! Men fighting in Lepanto!
Pirates in Roman times! Greek navigators!
Phoenicians, Carthaginians, Portuguese hurled out of Sagres
To boundless adventure on the Absolute Sea
          to realize the Impossible!
Hey there, hey there, hey. . .
You men who raised stone pillars to mark the
          coasts you discovered and named the capes!
Who first traded with the Negroes!
Who first sold slaves from new lands!
Who gave the astonished Negresses their first European orgasm!

You who brought back gold, glass beads, fragrant woods, arrows,
From coasts exploding with green vegetation!
You men who plundered peaceful African villages,
Scattering the natives with the roar of your cannon,
You who murdered, robbed, tortured, and grabbed the reward
Of the New Thing promised to those who lowered their heads
To rush out against the mystery of the new seas!
     Hey, hey, hey!
To all of you together, to all of you as though you were one,
To all of you mixed together and interlocking,
To all of you bloody, violent, hated, feared, revered,
I salute you, I salute you, I salute you!
Hey, hey, hey! Hey, hey, hey! Hey, hey, hey!
Hello there, hello there, hello, he . . . lloo . . . ooo!

I want to take off with you, I want to go away with you,
With all of you at once,
To every place you went!
I want to meet the dangers you knew face to face,
To feel across my cheeks the winds that wrinkled yours,
To split the salt sea that kissed your lips,
To pitch in with you as you work, to share the storms with you,
To reach like you, at last, extraordinary ports!
To flee with you from civilization!
To lose with you all moral sense!
To feel my humanity back off, silenced!
To drink with you in southern seas
New savageries, new tumults of the heart,
New central fires in my volcanic spirit!
To take off with you and leave behind—ah, come now,
     get in front of me!
—My civilized suit, my genteel behavior,
My innate fear of jails,
My peaceful life,
My sedentary, static, orderly, self-disciplined life!

To sea, to sea, to sea, to sea,
Hey there! put to sea, with the winds and the waves,
Oh my life!
With the foam on the winds
To salten my taste for great voyages,
With lashing torrents to whip my flesh to adventure,
Soak the bones of existence in freezing seas,
Flagellate, cut, and wrinkle with wind, sun, and foam
My cyclonic Atlantic being,
My nerves spread out like shroud ropes,
A harp in the hand of the winds!

Yes, yes, yes. . . Crucify me as you sail
And my shoulders will love the weight of the cross!
Bind me to each voyage as to a stake
And the pressure of the stake will pierce my spine
Till I feel it in one great passive orgasm!
Do what you want with me, so long as it's done at sea,
On deck, on top of the waves,
Wound me, kill me, tear me apart!
What I'd like is to bring to Death
A soul transformed by the Sea,
Dead drunk on everything having to do with the sea,
With sailors as much as with anchors and capes,
With far away coasts as much as with sounds,
With the Distant as with the Dock, with shipwrecks
As with run-of-the-mill shipping,
With masts as with waves,
And in voluptuous mourning, bring Death
A body swarming with leeches, sucking, sucking—
Those strange green absurd sea leeches!

Make shroud ropes out of my veins!
Hawsers out of my muscles!
Tear off my skin, nail it down to the keels,
Let me feel the pain of the nails and never stop feeling it!
Out of my heart make an admiral's flag
Unfurled in a battle between old sailing ships!

Let my ripped-out eyes be squashed underfoot on the decks!
Break my bones against hulls!
Tie me to masts and lash me, lash me!
Let the winds of all latitudes, longitudes,
Spread my blood over rushing waters
That dash side to side across poop decks
In the gale's rough caterwauling!

To be daring as cloth sails taut in the wind!
Like the high topsails in the whistling winds!
The old guitar, strumming a *fado* all about the perils at sea
A song for sailors to hear and never repeat!

The sailors who mutinied
Have hanged their captain from a yardarm.
Another they've left stranded on a deserted island.

Marooned!

The tropical sun has put the old pirate fever
In my burning veins.
The winds of Patagonia have tattoed on my imagination
Obscene and tragic images.
Fire, fire, oh fire inside me!
Blood, blood, blood, blood!
My skull explodes!
My world comes apart in crimson hunks,
My veins snap like clanking chains,
And out of me, fierce and voracious, bursts
The Great Pirate song,
The Great Pirate bellowing out his death knell,
His men below quaking with fear in their backbones,
And there on the quarterdeck amid the dying and shrieking,
        the singing:

> *Fifteen men on a Dead Man's Chest.*
> *Yo-ho-ho and a bottle of rum!*

Then the scream, in a voice grown unreal, shatters the air:

Darby M'Graw-aw-aw-aw-aw!
Darby M'Graw-aw-aw-aw-aw-aw-aw!
Fetch a-a-aft the ru-u-u-u-u-u-u-u-um, Darby!

Hey, that's the life, that was the life, ho! ho!
Ha-ha! ho-ho! ha-ha!
Hey there, hey there, that's it!

Crushed keels, sunk ships, blood on the waters,
Decks floating in gore, chunks of corpses!
Fingers lopped off on the gunwales!
Here and there, the heads of infants!
People with eyes gouged out screaming and howling!
Hey, that's it, hey, hey, hey!
Hey, that's it, hey, hey, hey!
I'm wrapped up in all this like a cape against the cold!
I rub up against all this like a cat in heat against the wall!
I roar through it all like a hungry lion!
I rush though it all like a mad bull!
I sink my nails, I tear my claws, I bloody my teeth
        through it all!
Hey, that's it, ho-ho, that's it!

My ears suddenly split—
It's like a great trumpet there at my side—
With that old cry, but raging, metallic now,
Calling out for its prize to show itself,
The schooner about to be taken:

Aho-o-o-o-o-o-o-o-o-o . . . yyy!
Schooner aho-o-o-o-o-o-o-o-o-o . . . yyyy!

For me the whole world comes to a stop! I'm red hot!
I roar in a frenzy to board her!
The Pirate Chief! King of the Pirates!
I pillage, I kill, I tear, I cut everything up!

All I feel is the sea—the seizure, the looting!
All I feel is the tom-tom of veins beating in me,
Beating my temples!
Hot blood drains out the sensation of having two eyes!
Hey-hey, that's it, that's it! Hey-hey-hey!

Ah, pirates, pirates, pirates!
Love me and hate me, pirates!
Pirates, let me melt into you!

Your cruel fury speaks to my blood
Of a woman's body that once was my own
And of which nothing is left but the sexual itch!

I want to be the beast
That acts out all your gestures,
That sinks its teeth in keels and gunwales,
That eats the masts and sops up blood and tar on deck,
That chews up sails and oars, ropes and pulleys.
A monster female sea serpent, glutting herself on crimes!

A symphony of sensations rises, incompatible and analogous,
An orchestration of tumultuous crimes, dinning in my blood,
Of spasmodic bloody orgies resounding on the sea,
Rising wildly like a hot gale in my soul,
A hot dust cloud dimming my lucidity,
Making me see and dream all this
          through my skin and veins only!

Pirates and piracy, ships and the moment,
That maritime moment when the prize is boarded
And the prisoners' terror approaches madness—that moment
With all its crimes, horror, ships, people, sea, sky, clouds,
Winds, latitude and longitude, outcries—
How I wish that in its allness it was my body
          in its allness, suffering,
My body and my blood, my whole being made one livid
          crimson glob
In bloom, like an itching wound, in the unreal flesh
          of my soul!

Let my passive body be the grand sum total woman of all women
Who were raped, killed, wounded, torn apart by pirates!
Let my violated body be that woman's who must serve them all!
And feel it all—feel all these things at once—in my backbone!

Oh, my heroes, coarse and hairy, adventurous and criminal!
My seafaring beasts, you husbands of my brain!
Quick lovers of my oblique sensations!
I'd love to be your One-and-Only awaiting you in every port,
You, the loved-and-hated pirates of her dreams!
Because she would be with you, though only in spirit, raped
Along with the naked corpses of your victims at sea!
Because she would be your accomplice in crime
        and in your oceanic orgies,
Her witch's spirit dancing invisibly amid the movements
Of your bodies, amid your cutlasses and your stranglers' hands!
And she, back on land, awaiting your return, if return you will,
She would drink in your roaring love,
        all the vast wide-openness,
All the fog-filled, sinister fragrance of your conquests
And during your orgasms she'd whistle the red-yellow *sabbath*
        of a black Mass!

Flesh torn, ripped open, disembowled, the blood pouring out,
Now, at the peak of my dream of your exploits,
I am totally lost; no longer belong to you, I *am* you,
My feminity, which accompanied you, become your very soul!
Now to be inside all your ferocity when you practice it,
Absorbing from within the feel of your sensations
When you stain the high seas with blood,
When occasionally you toss to the sharks
The still-living bodies of the wounded, the rosy flesh
        of children
And drag their mothers to the gunwales to watch it happening!

To be with you at the carnage and pillaging!
To be attuned to the symphony of your plundering!
Ah, I can't say, I can't tell you how much I'd love
        to be with you!

Not just be there as your women, be all women for you, be all
     your victims,
Being each and all victims—men, women, children, ships—
And not just be your opportune moment aboard ship
     and the waves,
Not just your souls, your bodies, your fury, your booty,
Not just being concretely your abstract orgiastic acts,
It's not just this that I want to be but, more than all this,
     be God of such Thisness!
I'd have to be God, I'd have to be God of some opposing faith,
A monstrous satanic God, a God of the blood's pantheism,
To come near satisfying the full extent
     of my imaginative frenzy
And never exhaust my desires to identify
With each and all and more-than-allness of your exploits!

Ah, torture me to cure me!
And this, my flesh—change it to that whoosh of air
     your slashing cutlasses make
Before they fall on heads and shoulders!
Change my veins to the threads of clothes
     your knives cut through!
My imagination to the woman's body that you violate!
My intelligence to the deck you stand on when you kill!
And make my whole life—nervous, hysterical, absurd
     kit-and-caboodle of it all—
Make it one huge organism with each act of piracy committed
One unit cell aware of it—and all of me whirling
Like one huge and undulating putrefaction—and let that be all!

In a sickening, immeasurable burst of speed,
The fever machine of my flooding visions
Now turns so that my consciousness in flight
Is scarcely more than a ring of smoke blown on the wind:

     Fifteen men on a Dead Man's Chest.
     Yo-ho-ho and a bottle of rum!

Hey there, hey there, ho-ho-ho, ha-ha-ha-ah-ah-ah . . .

Ah, the utter savagery of it all! Shit
On all life like ours that has nothing to do with it!
Here I am, an engineer, trained to use material energy,
    and aware of all its forms,
Here I am stalled, where you're concerned, even when
    I'm walking;
Inert, even when I act; weak, even when I impose myself!
Static, broken, dissident coward of your Glory,
Your great, strident, hot and bloody dynamism!

Damn it! for being unable to act out my madness!
Damn it! for always traipsing around, tied to the apron strings
    of civilization!
And going around burdened with my beautiful manners,
    like a load of lace on my back!
Hangers-on—that we all are—of modern humanitarianism!

Consumptives, neurasthenics, lymphatics in our languors,
Lacking the courage to be bold and violent men,
Dragging our soul behind like a chicken's leg tied by a string!

Ah, the pirates! the pirates!
The itch to do something illegal and savage,
The itch to do absolutely cruel abominable things,
Like an abstract rut gnawing our fragile bodies,
Our delicate feminine nerves,
Till great mad fevers burn in our empty gazes!

Let me always assume gloriously the submissive role
In bloody events and drawn-out sex bouts,
Fall on me like big heavy walls,
Oh barbarians of the ancient sea!
Tear me apart and maim me!
Going from east to west of my body,
Scratch bloody trails through my flesh!

Kiss with cutlass, boarding ax and frenzy
My joyous fleshy terror of belonging to you,
My masochistic itch to give in to your fury,
The sentient, inert object of your omnivorous cruelty—
Dominators, masters, emperors, corsairs!
Ah, torture me,
Slash me, rip me open!
As I lie broken in small, conscious pieces
Spill me across decks,
Scatter me over seas, leave me
On the islands' greedy beaches!
Gratify on me all the mysticism I have claimed for you!
Chisel your way through my blood to my soul!
Cut and tear!
Oh tattooers of my corporeal imagination!
Flayer-lovers of my bodily submission!
Subdue me like a dog you kick to death!
Make me the sewer of your scorn of mastery!
Make me all your victims!
Like Christ who suffered for mankind, I'd suffer
For every victim of your hands—
Calloused, bloody hands with fingers split
By your violent boardings at the gunwales!

Make of me a blob that has been
Dragged—oh my delight, oh kiss of pain!—
Dragged at the tail of horses you have whipped . . .
But all this on the sea—on the se-eeea, on the SE-EEEA!
Ho-ho-ho-hoho! Ho-ho-ho-ho—on the S-EE-EEA!

Yah-yah-yah! Yah-yah-yah-yah! Yah-yah-yah-yah-yah!
Everything screams! Everything is screaming!
      Winds, waves, ships!
Seas, topsails, pirates, my soul, blood, and the air, the air!
Ha-ha-ha—ha! Yah-yah-yah-yah! Yah-yah-yah-yah-yah-yah!
      Everything screaming and singing!

FIFTEEN MEN ON A DEAD MAN'S CHEST
YO-HO-HO AND A BOTTLE OF RUM!

Ha-ha-ha-ha-ha! Yah-yah-yah-yah! Yah-yah-yah-yah!
Ho-ho-ho-ho-ho! Hohohohohohoh! Ho-ho-ho-ho-ho!

AHO-O-O-O-O-O-O-O-O-O-O—yyy! . . .
SCHOONER AHO-O-O-O-O-O-O-O-O-O—yyy! . . .

Darby M'Graw-aw-aw-aw-aw-aw!
DARBY M'GRAW-AW-AW-AW-AW-AW-AW!
FETCH AFFFT THE RU-U-U-U-UM, DARBY!

Ho-ho-ho-ho-ho-ho-ho-ho-ho-ho-ho-ho-ho!
HO-HO-HO-HO-HO-HO-HO-HO-HO-HO-HO-HO-HO!
HO-HO-HO-HO-HO-HO-HO-HO-HO-HO-HO-HO-HO!
HO-HO-HO-HO-HO-HO-HO-HO-HO-HO-HO-HO-HO!
HO-HO-HO-HO-HO-HO-HO-HO-HO-HO-HO-HO-HO!

•   •   •

Something in me comes apart. A redness glows into dusk.
I've felt too much to go on feeling any more.
My soul is spent, an echo is all that's left inside me.
The flywheel slows down noticeably.
My dreams raise their hands a bit from over my eyes.
Inside I feel merely a vacuum, a desert, a nocturnal sea.
And as soon as I feel a nocturnal sea inside me
There rises up out of its distances, born of its silence,
Once more, once more, that vast, most ancient cry of all,
Suddenly as a light resounds with tenderness, not sound,
And instantly spreads all across the watery horizon,
The gloomy, humid surge of nighttime humanity,
A distant siren voice comes wailing, calling out,
From depths of Distance, Depths of Ocean, the center
        of Abysses,
While on the surface float like seaweed
        my dismembered dreams . . .

Aho-o-o-o-o-o-o-o-o-o—yy . . .
Schooner Aho-o-o-o-o-o-o-o-o-o-o-o-o—yy . . .

Ah, this light dew that covers my excitement!
This night-freshness out of my internal sea!
There it is, suddenly before me, a sea night
Full of the enormous human mystery of night waves.
The moon rises on the horizon
And my happy childhood stirs, like a tear, inside me.
My past surges back and that seafaring cry
Becomes a fragrance, a voice, the echo of a song,
As if to recall my childhood
And evoke that happiness that I can never know again.

It was in the old, quiet house along the riverside . . .
(The windows of my room, and the dining room too,
Look out past low-lying houses, over the nearby river,
Over the Tagus, this very Tagus, but from somewhere else,
            farther down . . .
If I returned to the same windows now I would not find
            the same windows.
That time has gone like a steamer's smoke on the high seas . . .)

An inexplicable tenderness,
A sad, a touching regret,
For all those victims—especially the children—
I dreamed of, imagining myself an old pirate,
A touching feeling, because they were my victims;
Gentle, soft—since they really weren't;
A confused tenderness, like a blurry windowpane turning blue,
Sings sad old songs in my poor sad soul.

Ah, how could I have thought and dreamt of such things?
How removed I am now from what I was a few minutes ago!
The hysteria of one's sensations—now one thing,
            now just the opposite!
Now in this pale morning light my hearing picks out
Those things in tune with this new emotion—the splash
            of the waters,
The light lapping waters as the river touches the docks . . .
The sails passing near the riverbank opposite,
The far-off hills in Japanese blue
Against the houses of Almada,
And all is gentle, newborn, in the early dawn hours . . .

A sea gull passes.
My tenderness increases.

Yet all this time I noticed nothing around me.
It was all something I felt on my skin, like a caress.
All this time I didn't take my eyes off my distant dream,
My house at the riverside,
My childhood by the river,
With the windows of my room looking out at the river at night,
And the peaceful moonlight spread over the waters . . .

My old aunt who loved me because of the son she'd lost . . .
My old aunt used to sing me to sleep
(Though I was already too grown up for lullabies) —
I recall this, and tears well up in my heart
            and cleanse my life,
And a light sea breeze rises inside me.
Sometimes she'd sing of "The Good Ship Catrineta":

> There goes the good ship Catrineta
> Over the sea and the waves.

Or that song, so nostalgic and medieval,
About "The Fair Princess" . . . I recall it now,
            and the poor woman's old voice stirs inside me,
Reminding me how little I've remembered since,
            and how much she loved me!
And how ungrateful I was to her . . . and finally,
            what have I done with my life?
"The Fair Princess" went . . . I'd close my eyes and she'd sing,

> As the fair princess
> Sat in her garden

I'd open my eyes a bit and see the window full of moonlight,
Then I'd shut my eyes again, so happy about it all.

> As the fair princess
> Sat in her garden,
> Combing her tresses,
> Her comb was golden . . .

Oh my childhood, a doll they broke for me!
I cannot go back to the past, that house
    and all that affection,
And stay there forever, forever a child and forever happy!

Well, it was all the Past, a lamppost on an old streetcorner.
To think of it makes me cold, hungry for what I can't have.
To think of it makes me absurdly, indefinably bitter.
Oh slow whirlwind of feeling, flying off in every direction!
Tenuous, vertiginous confusions of soul!
Spent rages, affections like spools of thread
    children play with,
The imagination collapsing in full gaze of all one's senses,
Tears, useless tears,
Light contrary winds grazing the soul . . .

To escape such feelings, I deliberately evoke,
By a desperate, dry, and empty effort of the will, I evoke
The song of the Great Pirate, about to die.

> *Fifteen men on a Dead Man's Chest.*
> *Yo-ho-ho and a bottle of rum!*

But the song fades like a poorly traced straight line
    inside me . . .

I force myself again, and succeed in calling up
    before my gazing soul
Again, though through the medium of
    a semiliterary imagination,
The pirates' fury, love of slaughter, appetite,
    and almost physical taste for plunder . . .
The pointless slaughter of women and of children,
The useless torture of the poor passengers,
    only to amuse themselves,
And the lust to smash those things most cherished
    by the others,
But as I dream all this I'm afraid of something
    breathing down my neck.

I remember how interesting it would be
To hang children before their mothers' eyes
(Though involuntarily feeling I'm the children's mothers),
To bury four-year-olds on desert islands,
Rowing their fathers up to see it done
(Though it makes me shudder, recalling a child I never had,
        peacefully asleep at home.)

I incite a cold passion for crimes at sea,
An Inquisition with no excuse of Faith,
Crimes with no motive, not even malice and anger,
Done in cold blood, not even to hurt or do wrong,
Not for a joke, but just to kill time,
Like someone playing solitaire at the dinner table
        in the country, the tablecloth pushed to one side
        after dinner,
Just for the fun of committing abominable crimes
        and not thinking twice about it,
Just to see someone suffer, go crazy and dying of pain,
        yet never letting it come to that point . . .
But my imagination refuses to follow me.
A chill makes my hair stand on end,
And suddenly (more suddenly than before, more distant
        and more profound in suddenness)
—oh the fright that freezes my veins!—all of a sudden
That sudden cold as the door to the Mystery opens inside me
        and lets in a draft!
I remember God, the Transcendent-in-life, and suddenly
The old voice of the British sailor Jim Barnes with whom I used
        to talk,
Becomes now inside me the voice of mysterious endearments,
        with all those little details of being
        in my mother's lap and my sister's hair-ribbon,
But now stupendously borne from the other side
        of the appearance of things,
The deafening, far-off Voice become the Absolute Voice,
        the Mouthless Voice,
Borne from the surface and depths
        of the sea's nocturnal Solitude,
Calling me, calling me, calling me . . .

It comes through muffled, as though stifled but still audible,
From far far away, as though sounding elsewhere
        and not hearable,
Like a smothered cry, a doused light, a silenced breath.
From no point in space, from no place in time,
The everlasting night cry, the deep, confusing exhalation:

        Aho-o-o-o-o-o-o-o-oo———yyy . . .
        Aho-o-o-o-o-o-o-o-o-o-o———yyy . . .
        Schooner aho-o-o-o-o-o-o-o-o-o-oo—yy . . .

A cold shiver passes through my body from the depths of my soul
And I quickly open my eyes that I hadn't closed.
Ah, what joy coming out of my dreams at once!
Here's the real world again, so good for the nerves!
Here's the early morning with its newly arrived ship
        entering the port.

Which ship has arrived doesn't matter a bit.
        It's still far off.
Only what's close-up now warms the heart.
Now it's my imagination, strong, practical, hygienic,
That busies itself only with modern and useful things,
With freighters, steamships and passengers,
With powerful, immediate, modern, commercial,
        down-to-earth things.
The flywheel inside me slows down.

Wonderful modern maritime life,
Everything so sanitary, mechanized, healthy!
Everything so well regulated, so spontaneously adjusted,
All the cogs and wheels, all the ships at sea,
All facets of mercantile enterprise, export and import,
So marvelously managed
That everything runs as if by natural law,
Nothing jarring or out of place!

Poetry hasn't lost out a bit. Moreover, we now have
      the machine
With its own poetry as well, and a totally new way of life,
Businesslike, worldly, intellectual, sentimental,
Which the machine age has endowed our souls with.
Voyages are now as beautiful as they ever were,
And a ship will always be beautiful, simply because
      it's a ship.
A sea voyage is still a sea voyage and distance exists
      where it always did—
Nowhere, thank God!
Seaports full of steamships of every conceivable type!
Large and small, and all painted differently, each
      with its distinct schedule of watches for its crew,
Each one exquisitely following the choice of one
      of so many companies!
Each steamer in port so unique in its well-marked mooring!
So festive in the quiet elegance of its commercial traffic
      on the seaways,
Over the always ancient Homeric seaways, oh Ulysses!

The humanitarian glance of the lighthouses far out at night
Or the sudden glare of the lighthouse beam nearby
      on a dark thick night
("How close we must now be to land!" And the water sings
      in our ears)! . . .

All this today is what's always been,
      except that there's trade,
And the commercial purpose of the great ships
Makes me boast of this age I live in!
The variety of people aboard passenger ships
Fills me with the modern pride of living in an age
      when it's so easy
For races to come together, cover distances, and see all
      the new things so easily,
Thus making real and enjoying in one's lifetime
      a great many things only dreamt of before!

Clean, adjusted, and modern as an office of counters enclosed
    in yellow wire netting,
My feelings now are ordinary and respectable as *gentlemen,*
Being practical and wholly undistracted, they fill the lungs
    with sea air,
Like people perfectly aware of how salubrious it is
    to inhale sea air.

Now the day starts perfectly as a working day.
It all gets under way, everything falling into place.
With great pleasure, natural and straightforward, I recite
    by heart
All the commercial operations needed to get a shipment of goods
    on its way.
My age is the rubber stamp appearing on all invoices
And I feel that all letters in all offices
Must be addressed to me.

A knowledge of shipping is so distinctive,
And a ship captain's signature is so beautiful and modern!
The strict commercial style of beginning and ending a letter:
Dear Sirs—Messieurs—Amigos e Srs.,
Yours faithfully— . . . *nos salutations empressées* . . .
It's all not only human and tidy but also beautiful,
And it's all finally got a maritime purpose—
    the vessel with freight
Being shipped is what the letters and invoices are about.

Life's complexity! Invoices are made out by men
Who love and hate, have political passions,
    sometimes commit crimes—
And their invoices are so well written, so perfectly aligned,
    so independent of all that!—
There are those who can look at an invoice and not feel this
    at all.
Surely you, Cesário Verde, you once felt this.
As for me, I feel it so personally I can almost weep.
Don't tell me there's no poetry in business, in offices!

Why, it seeps through every pore . . . I breathe it in the sea air
Because it's all got to do with ships and modern navigation,
Because invoices and commercial letters are the beginnings
        of history,
And ships carrying goods on the everlasting sea are its end.

And, ah, the voyages, the holiday cruises, and the rest,
The sea voyages where we all get to be fellow passengers
In a special way, as though some mystery of sea custom
Had touched our hearts and momentarily changed us
Into traveling compatriots of some indeterminate fatherland,
Forever changing location on the vast ocean!
Grand Hotels of the Infinite, oh my transatlantic liners!
With the totally perfect cosmopolitanism of never stopping
        at any point
And encompassing every type of costume, countenance, and race!

Voyages and voyagers—and so many different types of them!
So many nationalities on earth, so many professions,
        so many people!
So many different directions to steer one's life,
And life itself, in the end and at heart, always the same!
So many strange faces! All faces are strange
And nothing gives one the sense of what's holy
        so much as watching people constantly.
Brotherhood isn't finally a revolutionary idea,
It's something you learn by living your life,
        when you've got to tolerate everything,
And where you begin finding pleasant
        what you've got to tolerate,
And you end up nearly weeping with tenderness
        over the things you tolerate!

Ah, and all this is beautiful, all this is human
        and firmly tied up
To the life of feelings—so human, so sociable, so bourgeois,
So complexly simple, so metaphysically sad!
Drifting, diverse, life ends by teaching us to be human.
Poor people! Poor people, all of us, everywhere!

I take leave of this moment in the shape of this other ship
Setting out now. It's an English *tramp steamer,*
Filthy enough to be French,
With the homely look of a seafaring proletarian,
And listed no doubt on the last page
      of yesterday's shipping-news.

The poor ship touches me, it moves so humbly and naturally.
There's a certain scrupulousness about it—in what way
      I can't say—like an honest person
Going about doing whatever he has to do.
Now it's moving away from the dock in front of me,
      from the spot where I'm standing.
There it goes quietly by where caravels used to go by
Long ago, long long ago . . .
Headed for Cardiff? Liverpool? London?
      It doesn't matter where.
It's doing its job. Like us doing ours.
      Life is so beautiful!
Bon voyage! Bon voyage!
Bon voyage, poor passing acquaintance, you did me the favor
Of sharing with you the fever and fret of my thoughts,
And bringing me back to life so I could think of you
      and watch you go by.
Bon voyage! Bon voyage! That's what life is . . .

Your poise is so natural, so inevitably matutinal,
Leaving Lisbon harbor today,
You fill me with a curious familiar affection for . . .

For what? Well, I know what's out there! . . . But go ahead . . .
      pass by . . .
With a slight shudder
(T-t—t——t———t . . .)
The flywheel inside me stops.

Slow ship, pass by, pass away and don't stop . . .
Leave me, pass way out of sight,
Take yourself out of my heart,
Vanish in the Distance, the farthest Distance, the Mist of God,
Disappear, follow your destiny, leave me behind . . .
Who am I to weep and ask questions?
Who am I to speak to you and love you?
Who am I to be upset by the sight of you?
It leaves the dock, the sun rises, turns golden,
The roofs of buildings along the dock begin to glow,
This whole side of the city is sparkling . . .
Goodbye now, leave me—first be
The ship in midriver, standing there bright and clear,
Then, the ship passing the sandbar, small and black,
Then, a vague speck on the horizon (oh my dread!),
A speck growing vaguer and vaguer on the horizon . . .
Then, nothing at all—only me and my sorrow,
And now a great city full of sunlight,
And this moment, real and bare as a deserted dock,
And the slow-moving crane that turns like a compass
Tracing a semicircular course of God knows what emotion
In the compassionate stillness of my heart . . .

EVACUATION

CHARLES HENRI FORD

1

Ill-treated city, up to nothing in particular, what goes with your pestilence supplies? Away from you, we feel compressed, like a porcelain photostat.

Stalled all day on a perforated snowplow, the mayor said, "May I be delivered from night baseball!" Something's gone wrong with his moral support. Previews have him enveloped in a nimbus of noise.

Eighteen ornithologists agree: "Most protoplasmic fiction is pointless all the way." Other emaciated panelists repeat: "The working classes have little time for parlor-car furnishings."

Have you been in my block recently? Through the peephole of nonsecrets, everything is making it the piston rod way. Implausible at best, except in a flick, we'd rather it came out simulated. How about that retake, a one-way paraphrase—"as yawning sounds break through the food circuit barrier."

All of which means, behind self-carrying putrefaction, there's more dilation in store for cunts.

An obscure paper hanger was astonished to find himself on pantheistic grazing ground. What happens on safer pathways? Like I said, a papier-mâché police dog don't get nosebleed.

Do you want to be a marooned pyromaniac, getting off his kernels in Potter's Field? You're not in Never Before, you're at Ever After. During peak perturbation carnivores sneak home.

For my pock-marked barber (angular eyewitness) a ductile headdress reaching to hipbone level . . . When the dawn patrol of Pre-existence opens its magneto mouth, it's a piercing good night.

2

A clean break with the past is—how not to be tormented. To pile up rooftop morale and become a legend by the time you're nowhere. "Amen!"

Sex fiends make full use of their hidden antennae. Love-making in a rickety spacecraft is very trippy. No way back. The afternoons are a little peculiar. Who loves who? In an iridescent room at Marienbad, Sis found out.

When you do it together, it needn't be as amoral as all that. Still, never carry more cash than you can afford to lose.

Now this cruel reunion in Nashville. The Fallen Race . . . One had lots of blond hair. They move, they eat, they breed. Pretty sneaky, Ivan!

Our greasy Bard, heir to an aristocratic tradition, went on and on: ". . . Sure I sweat, but your psyche lets you know—c'est ça le miracle . . ." Exit a man and his tapeworm.

Hendrix, busted in Toronto, achieved exaltation. He's not the only maharajah wears bonnets of the Unbelievable.

3

Moreover, a double-life stewardess was never meant to terrorize enemies within. Sputum-flow, our national sport, is not saving money at all. At speeds rivaling the prismatic trickle of a losing streak, many fishy policemen screeched on campus. Objective? Which one will spook an integrated, automated, rather in-between Colored Man.

What's wrong? You get what you spit on. Much conversation is dementia-prone, with expressions such as "no-haste punk stink" and "syphilitic synagogue sellout." Unfulfilled seamen spread their own snotty clobber. The winner? An involved slave girl with hairless pink slit. Or maybe somebody else's pelvis-power swami. This unnamed Victrola replacement ought to squawk "Sugar Blues."

An old unorthodox spiritualist thinks about spectral motion pictures (not for sale to the Armed Forces). Self-centered Sodomy, it's your move.

4

My elephant-driver's got this aversion to furlike relationships. His heart's a drive-in glacier, pining for liquefaction. No one else stands up to the mailman's pulpy irradiation.

Some half-wit found in the hallway begins to scrape pale carrots, misshapen as interbred penises. An extinct draftee will catch it. Get your hands on the Master Key! Then start the Incoherence Generator. From our arsenal of incongruity any kind of molecule will do. In the molten enclosure invertebrates gather, like Brutalism disemboweled.

A cyclist on the road to Vermilion Gulch (where internal piles get reborn) seems about to explode. The magistrate's megaphone knows it's blues time. A local masochist slips inside their shelter-in-the-mire; licorice blackjacks melt in his mouth. "Suck a blackjack for peace!"

Can you, Comrade, dance the Mongol Crunch? Mr. Gooey Splotch, unmuzzled machinist with crash diaphragm, wore a bladder of moire.

The next begrimed forearm you kiss needn't overpower. Inaudible as the interlacing roots of a flashback artesian well, cyclonic as the absurd rhetoric of great poetry, we rise . . . and dissect.

5

Since when is it easier to unload in funky grammar school? Foulmouthed aristocrats give you the facts, like, man, the malodorous chain reaction from CIA files.

Remember the nothing rash you had last year? St. Onan does not bristle all alone; his conic fluid shows that, with hotbed sediment, cranial overtones eventually become as fictionized as the Highway Code.

Our good night catalyst of disposable gauze would neutralize the offshoot. *"Always serve hot with a fresh contagion sauce and gillpod salad."* A pleasant change from sperm-white layer cake.

One of your joker friends, Bo Bumwell, alias The Ooze, or so the legend goes, found a bigger one to be at fault. Fall in love with clabber-cold Ophelia? Her inactive volcano, overdeveloped as a mollusk raised to inalienable menstruation, was temptingly close, like a last-act nebula winging away. The nastiest backdrop garniture, makeshift adhesive of nameless procreation, had to be a royal occasion, thrilling as the sight of a thunderstorm from a crosstown bus.

6

In the tilt-table room for physiological testing there's a bucktoothed childwife stuck with instant-replacement wearing apparel. Ready or not, kicky exhalations will get to her. She's handcuffed with an amulet Valentino's janitor found on the floor of the dead-letter office. On her lips, color of grasshoppers' eyes, a taste of codeine. Her dazed and unsure adductor (Eunuch of Benedictions), during a crotch-oriented rodeo in Affinity Gap, ate some odd berries; he doesn't believe anymore in lunar takeover. Plantlike leavings are beckoning upward.

Lying within reach, the clammy locomotive of unutterable glut becomes his kind of divination. Like an amphibian in dungarees, he no sooner has it out than gentle-suction configuration shows in three fluoroscopes. Hands off the eight-legged day laborer! Antagonist composed of fiery substances, he wants to tell you about chemical toilets and the first spectographic lab this side the creamery.

Twelve centuries from now, in a domain of abandoned crags, orgiastic rites discharge their hay-sweet sap. Only you, architect of alliteration, with the speed of sound, will write your own ending. On the Trans-Asian Express, there's the nonsexual clot to be decoded, nocturnal emissions on a rhythmic scale.

The Pope is about to visit Africa, to mourn an engulfed battalion and to purchase foot spray for airtight confessionals. A hairy veil hangs over the unexplored Atlantic.

7

From this rewind, her impersonation of a cave dweller in sequined tulle will not be easily forgotten by Ursula Andress. Scaley female mammal lingering in what unreal quagmire . . . O tremulous profanation!

Condemned to shadowy turmoil, the Yalta Conference quadrupeds rap about the uterus. In the same zoological garden, quivering zealots in light blue stockings form venereal linkings. Repulsively transfigured, a destitute crew surrounds them, unavoidable as a locust swarm. Subcutaneous tracery reappears. The tide, like a Biblical epic of Undesirables, is rising.

For buggery in the vestry there's no zero hour. A visionary straggler in Artic regions stretches out beside me. Unbalanced as second nature, an unzipped vivisectionist finds himself aghast, whilst agate-eyed Eros is sweeping the sidewalk.

At the Point of No Return, normal calculations replace the spikes of vermin. O squashy yams of reverie! You may as well uncurl; lice and fleas get thirsty on long trips. So does a misunderstood former child star.

8

O garnet-studded afterbirth!

The compulsory lanterns of ourselves are being taken down. Outpost ulcerations have arrived. Your cruising altitude, Gringo, is like smoking a carbon paper goofbutt. You were not meant to groove on heights of glory. Every time you gurgle, hothouse appendages appear; flame-throwers at eventide are flecked with gossamer body tissues. In the gloaming, like a convent quickening with roaches and handjobs, the excavation of a 1932 luncheonette . . .

What started it all—while deciphering an excrescence, I overheard one of the inmates whisper: "Creamed codfish sent by boat is not my idea of languishment-speckled gratification." His gawky adversary slipped me a tab: "Tonight in the Forgery Arcade . . ." Protective excretions are not enough. On the esplanade, inflammable plumage of silent insolence is flaunted by a wading bird.

FIVE SONNETS

WILLIAM BRONK

LOVE AS A GREAT POWER

It seems there is almost nothing but it could do:
stop wars, make ugliness beautiful,
injustice level, hungriness full

—or fullness hungry: a force that changes things.
Can we say that wide is broad, extension length,
or anything itself after the change,

—that there is a nature of things, a reality?

And we yield to it, give ourselves over, as though
a name were called and it were our name
and we call out another and hear the answer come.

Then it goes. Incredible. It leaves us. We are left.
Unexpectedly nothing. We listen; have nothing to call.
We wonder how we could ever have used that name.

Now, we are not. Love is a great power.

TALKS WITH THE EMISSARIES

It is sleep which takes us aside and offers to.
And the offer tempts us; we are susceptible,
have known sleep for a long time, can recall
things it brought us even without promises.

But our special openness—what sleep may know—
is our knowledge these last few days confirmed, that what
we see or do, in the ordinary way,
in the day's course is just not there,

doesn't matter, is beside the point, real,
in the sense of actual and factual if you believe that,
but the most trivial, indifferent kind of fact.

There is a stranger, farther place we belong to, too,
and sleep has ways it knows to get us there.
I haven't dared what death might have to say.

SOMETHING MATTERS BUT WE DON'T

In man, I can see no substance solidly;
it is as if what we call man were no more
than an oddly-angled look at something else.
Or is it my limitation, being man,
not to be able to see whatever is there?
And aren't these two alternatives the same?

Let me leave off speaking, unknowing as I am,
but not before I speak of the limits of speech,
or tell of man there is nothing to tell,
or tell of what we discern perhaps there could be
to tell that we know too little except it is there
and, if anything happens, it must be it happens there

and not to us, not by us; good
or evil, it doesn't matter what we do.

DOS–à–DOS

We aren't face to face. What is there to hide?
Nothing. The trouble is there's nothing to hide.
Is there something to keep? We haven't kept.

My face was open to you. You looked at it.
I looked in your open face. What there is I saw.
Don't look now. Nothing is hidden there.

Turn your back away. Go round. Go round.
What did you see when you looked at me? *Gent*
go round the lady and lady go round the gent.

Mirror my emptiness as you found it there.
Then in the empty mirror, mirror me.
Let the mirror be covered as in the house of the dead.

Back off. Perform our figures at will: *gent*
go round the lady and lady go round the gent.

HIS POEMS

To say I only listen isn't true
but neither is it conversation really: in the end
whatever is said is theirs. If I hold back,
their stubborn assurance, their patience, waits for me.

It might be a long wait; apart from the times
I fight them, there are times I wasn't even wrong.
I discover later what they said. Or, prompted by that,
I look for other things they, maybe, could say.

There are some they hold back: answers I want
to questions it would do me no good to ask. And I don't.
Not really. But I want to know. Are the answers there?

Alone sometimes, I remember how certain things
were said: that's what we were talking about
and the statement was made that—and then, oh! Yes!

SIX POEMS

CARL RAKOSI

AMERICANA 6

Captain Patterson, the folks back home
would like to know how you feel
about your first kill.

We had just completed our mission
and were rolling out when we saw four MIG-17S
off our left wing.
                    They headed towards us
so we jettisoned our tanks
                              and blew our afterburners
and climbed left.
                    The lead MIG started firing.
The fight was on.
                    I put our Phantom into a 70° dive.
One MIG crossed our canopy from right to left,
leaving the area at a good speed.
I was about to take off after him
when another MIG appeared at 10 o'clock high.
"That's our baby,"
                    I called to Doug.
"Let's get him on the radar."
                              He locked in
and for three miles we were in trail.

Then we closed in and fired the sidewinder
real smooth off our left wing.
For a long while it just trailed the MIG,
then delicately at about a thousand feet behind
it straightened out and sailed into his tailpipe.
Blew him into a brilliant fire ball.

It was a piece of cake.
                        We wish they'd come up
and say hello more often.

FIDDLING A ROUND

Go, imagination,
doodle,
        run amuck
while I am fiddling
desperately for a theme.
Distract me
            from my authentic self.
Show what you can do
with a lowly word like *fiddling*.

"I would rather hear
a roomful of aldermen
fiddling over a tavern license
than a writer fiddle on his grandiosity"

Bravo!

or "It's time you came, Orpheus,
to our steel tombs
and expelled all this intellectual fiddling."

I'll drink to that.

"Give me the fiddling in a fairy ring
                              of fern"

Lovely. Positive it!

"and a fortuity of fiddling."

Now that's a horse
                    of another fiddle.

"There's an existence of fiddles
perched like birds on a high
                              power line"

A hit! a palpable!

"and isn't the grasshopper's fiddle akimbo?"

That could put me into stitches
if it had a thread.

Consider also
              "awake to viols
              but condemned to fiddle"

ah, the human condition!

or "the poor beggar doesn't have
  a fiddle to his obvious."

Who does?

Now to the bass string:

"The country fiddles
                      while the emotion burns
and The Great Powers
                      convene."

Now *there* is fiddling!
a tale of vice versa,
the fiddling of a battle
                of jaws,
or of instant history
as when the emperor of Rome cried, "Let her burn!"

and finally "Einstein's infinite
                    fiddle."

Ah, I could lay me down in such a featherbed
and travel to Alpha Centauri on an imaginary number.

"But where are the fiddles of Israel?"

Aleph the ox in Hebrew takes a grave measure.
Let us play it like we feel.

And where are the scribblings
                    of yesteryear?

fiddled away! fiddled away!

AMERICANA 1924

They learned first how to handle a rifle
and went into the woods
for squirrel and pheasant
and hooked bait
with the care of a paleontologist.

At night they sat with whisky
and said to a companion
                    "Let's get drunk"
and the answer came back
                      "All right."

When they went to war and were afraid
and got shot up
and found a girl and had a family

or shot lion and climbed Kilimanjaro
and pursued the dark Iberian
                              gored
Who sighted with his sword
the place of death
                    behind the bull's neck
and went in over the horns,
holding back nothing,
all they had to say was
                    "It's good
when the fall rains come"
and the answer was
                    "Swell."

Will there be no more larks
                    or Cezanne's apples?
Adieu then.

ERE-VOICE

"Who is there
            to attain What?"
the master of Ch'an
            the medium of the ocean

FOUR-PART INVENTION FOR THE ORGAN

Origen gapes
                and would speak.
Speak!
        Are you tormented?
I hear the stone of sound.
Deus in reeds.
                    Titans sob.
From the mouth of Okeanus
to the orifice of chaos
it verberates and roams,
its destiny never
to enter matter.
Hence its pitch is off.
Not bad for souls.
So beautiful is matter,
souls are purified
and punished there.

Old cloud chamber.
Origen cut his balls
                    off there.
All dead,
        old theologies.
No more listeners.
Old dead.
Still it speaks.
Neither sorrow nor the absence of it,
only apprehension
which freezes souls
and hangs them from a beam
where they can only bound
on air currents.

Again it speaks
as from a crater
dry and angry,
breath of dogma.
Quake, limbs!
Open, bowels!
Logos is
Gnosis is
Origen is°

A MUSTACHE DRAWN ON AMERICANA 6

I'll bet you dollars to doughnuts
the Vincents hit us tonight.
The village chief just took off,
claiming he had business in Danang.

I'd like to take off myself,
all the way to Flint, Michigan.
For openers I'd show up at the airport
with a big sign, GET THE MARINES OUT OF VIETNAM.
Under that in smaller letters:

                              starting with me.

°Origen is believed to have castrated himself in order to reach the
pure state necessary for teaching Christianity to woman.

PORFIRI AND ESTHALINA

DENNIS SILK

PART 1

Porfiri Uspenski landed at Jaffa in 1853. This self-denying Archi-
mandrite ("I an unworthy priest") had ferried his Russians to
Palestine. These icon-kissers sat on the quayside. They smelt of
bilge, they would carry it up to Jerusalem. Wrapped in clouts,
they sang their pilgrim songs. They supped in Jaffa. They up-
ended the breadsacks carried from their villages. They sliced away
the nasty mold, they got down to good Russian sense, they pushed
the real substantial bread round the cabbage soup.

Porfiri smiled on them. But he could smack his own face or
shout at the Uspenski that saved him from Porfiri. Scandal to a
hermitage. And then a kind of pointless boredom. It rained again,
today. Dear Lady of Novgorod, save me. Another letter from the
Procurator.

His days passed, bearlike and important. He was thirty-eight,
perhaps he wanted to die. He was beached, with the pilgrims, at
Jaffa.

Partisan
The escort sent by the Pasha of Jerusalem raised such a dust. It
worried the Virgin. Her banner flicked the horsemen. A partisan of
hers talked up at them. Ishmael on horseback. Please understand
they're our escort, Porfiri said to this loon. He must have gnawed
through the rope tethering him to his bed. Stable of Ishmael. We'll

scrape away your dung in Hagia Sophia. A horseman lit a cigarette. Yes, and clap our hands for the Tsar of Constantinople, in Tsargrad, smoking a cigarette in the name of all the Russian princes. With his right hand he crossed himself, he stood in the restored Hagia Sophia, himself a prince to the grateful Greeks there. It was shaming to observe, with his left he conveyed Porfiri's handkerchief to his own pocket.

The Way

Banners of the Lady form. Very pious soldiers sustain Our Lady of Novgorod, Our Lady of Vladimir, the Virgin of Three Hands. Very tidy, very correct. Her serious soldiers learn the way. Then Greeks and Armenians. That's not good. But monks, anyway. Then the pilgrim army. And Porfiri Uspenski voluble with his Consul-General from Beirut.

Her banner over Ramleh. Sour ankles stumble through Ramleh. Raggedy Russians under the moon. They cram the pass. Patrol the defile. Lots of medals. Lots of moon. When the banditti see all those medals they scuttle home again. The Armenians breathe again.

Pilgrims pray. Lady of the Way, shine for us. Garnish our soup. Lady of the Knout, the Cudgel, under our mold your white.

Regimentals

Old soldiers in regimentals under the moon. Sebastopol to Jerusalem. The moon's pulley jerks the soldiers. Lèft right lèft the Virgin says. Keeps them in good order. Unlettered puppets smile. Pleased by her soup at every station. The caravan of the Russians approaches Jerusalem. Three times round the wall the puppets creak. Spectators clap.

Porfiri feels like a trick puppet glazed by the moon. He takes off his Uspenski head, and offers it to the spectators up there. Under the top head a Porfiri head, almost his own it seems, with a set expression picked up on the way. A Porfiri set look at the town, an intelligent forecast. The silly Uspenski head orbits round the moon.

Two silly soldiers stare up at the town. They're beyond hope. They're on the town. One head each, two together if you count the two of them. Regimental mathematics. They're drill-drunk, cabbage-drunk, soup-drunk. Poor Lady to have such partisans. Lèft right lèft right and so into town.

Turnips

Turnip pilgrims scowl at the town. Here's the tout for the icon-seller, the conserver of the last milk of the Virgin (extremely nourishing), the informer rare plant of Novgorod, the handkerchief bandit, the color-sergeant who stole from his comrades, the simplifier from the Theological College at Minsk. They burn their farthing candles to the moon.

Family

Whose faces under the moon? Cramming the parapet? Porfiri counts his dead. Town walls stuffed with his dead. Cousins, second cousins, the family-likenesses signal him on. A clink of medals— the old soldiers acknowledge his dead. It's Russia all right. The Dnieper encircles Jerusalem. But the Lady of Vladimir has deserted her banner. She conducts a choir of dead sisters hymning him from the battlement. Eyes closed, she keeps good time. A tattered Orthodox hymnal flutters up there. They sing Porfiri in. Boots of the pilgrims clutter Jaffa Gate.

PART 2

Name Day

Metropolitan Filaret held a reception. It was the name day of the Tsar, all the Patriarchs and Consuls were invited. The Bashi-Bazouks discharged their cannon. You had to be in Jerusalem at that moment, you had to see the exultation of the people.

A Turkish band tried out a Russian tune. Filaret sent it down lemonade. Porfiri looked at that lidded face in the window. A spinning top finding its way round top. Bishop Nikon didn't look like that. The thin mind of Filaret and the thick mind of Nikon. Somehow to steer between.

The terms of his mission were hardly defined. To study the pilgrims, make recommendations. Their piety, their politics. Swaddled children sent out by the princes.

Nikon came over to point out the Patriarchs. Moodily fending off some missionary lady, Anba Basilius the Copt. All the way from Cairo, to push out the Ethiopians. A matter of the status quo. Status quo? That means holding on to everything you've got. They brought in a burnt sugar savory. Rights and sites, he added grimly. Costive in a corner, Bishop Joseph the Ethiopian. He *never* talks to Basilius. And it's all to do with the key to a chapel. Copts and robbers, Filaret calls it. Who's that? said Porfiri. In a green cloak, with embroidered lions. That's Ozoro Esther the Ethiopian princess. Black and bored she looked out through a window. That's the young widow. I consider her a penitent woman, said Nikon. He inspected the new tray. Sherbet and caviar, ecumenical treat, for the Tsar's name day.

Filaret on the Status Quo

There was a Latin who hadn't strayed from his site in the Sepulchre for years. Maybe he was afraid, if he did, the Greeks one night would roll it up like a carpet. So he stayed there, loyal to the Latins, perpetually fed as it were by the Eucharist. One day he visited the Armenian section, he was very imprudent, he thought no one was looking. He went round interestedly inspecting, fingering rather, the hangings, the fixtures, everything that could be fingered after years of deprivation.

Matin

Nikon conducted thickly. Unworthy Porfiri, lighting a candle. In all indolence he looked toward the Royal Doors, prayed first of all for his charges and next his own sins. The Mother's eyes on the Iconostasis, to take him through. Not all the saints, not all that light. He thought of her, in the stable, knees drawn up, fighting in dark against her pain, her Child. "Glory to thee, God-chosen Mother, Mother of God, Queen of Heaven and earth, glory to Thee." After Mass, nothing to note but an old nun at a lectern, reading to herself in a questioning tone.

Breakfast

The sun again, today. Porfiri fool. Hat and beard and boredom. At breakfast he had the look of a sly wooden horse. Filaret considered him thinly. A spinning top's whipped early in the morning. Porfiri lumbered into religion.

They breakfast on itineraries. Nikon thinks well of Christ. The Virgin, too. This Tomb, and that Tomb. A Patriarch, or so, to throw in, also. Over their heads portraits of Tsar Alexi and his friend the Patriarch. (Attraction of wood.) To sound Joseph on the status quo.

Then there's the serious business of the pilgrims. A panorama, or two.

Virgin's Tomb

Oil lamps going all the way down to the Virgin. A little Armenian angel on the first lamp, a Greek cross on the second. Alternating, all the way down. Sweet little status quo.

An angel. And no devil. No, he twined himself round the status quo. Status quo, the High God of this town.

The Son snuggled up to the Virgin in an icon glassed against theft. Of paste? The real jewels were at the Greek Patriarch's. Vague eyes down there. Money-dreams, Virgin-dreams, who knew?

Theology

Bishop Joseph looked insecure in his tatty court. He sat in his tiny chair, maybe it had been made for a deacon, next to his real chair in gilt. Occupied, it would have forced him to straighten his back. Chairs crowded his walls as if for a tribal gathering. Above, prints or photos of the royal line: Theodoros uses a lion as a cosy mat, Johannes, Zauditu.

Softly he began to ask Porfiri about the Bible. Were there records, outside it, of the Jews through from Adam to Herod? Maybe he thought the Russian Church possessed a secret archive of these events. It surprised Porfiri anyone in Jerusalem wanted to engage in religious discussion. Bishop Joseph sensed his surprise. Forgive these questions, he said defensively. A match has a head, you strike it. A man should talk things over, shouldn't be alone. He seemed alone enough there. A little Ethiopian warmth, much loneliness, among chairs.

Bishop Joseph was said to be in love. He'd a new robe for Easter sewn by a seamstress. She came many days to the Convent, he didn't discourage her. When she'd finished, he asked her to stay. All the coffers of Ethiopia couldn't persuade.

On the Roof

Mountainy Ethiopian monks guarded the door to the staircase to their chapel. With knives and sticks. They'd used them. One of them had hit a Copt with a crucifix. The Ethiopian deacon had got his key back. He waved it maliciously. The Coptic guardian scowled. When Anba Basilius hears, he'll send such a letter to Cairo.

Bishop Joseph got his deacon to unlock the door for Porfiri. He led down his new Russian friend to the Chapel of the Four Bodiless Living Creatures. Peeling on the wall they stared down at Porfiri. A Russian, perhaps? At any rate, not an Armenian. Not a Copt. Terrible disrepair of the Creatures. For the party that possessed the Chapel repaired it. Its possession disputed, no one repaired it.

Virgin and Son glowed in a curtained icon. Chaste neglect, here. In Virgin's Tomb, wanton exposure. On the wall Porfiri noticed an inscription in Arabic. He pointed it out, demurely, to Joseph. Evidence of Coptic possession? Very few Ethiopians knew Arabic. He'd had to filter his own bad Arabic, his Novgorod Arabic, to Joseph through a dragoman. Oh yes, said Joseph, a little lamely it seemed to Porfiri, so soon as the Copts see some Arabic on a wall, or on an icon, they say, that's our wall, our icon. Arabic's Coptic, they say. But oh if we have something in Arabic, that they don't like.

After a cooling patrol of the Chapel battlefield, they climbed back to the heat of the roof. Here the Ethiopian monks and nuns had their little kraal. Deir-as-Sultan. Africa, almost, in Jerusalem. Forced out from the Sepulchre below, because of their indigence, they'd lived two centuries on its roof. So many loaves of bread a day, doled out by the Armenians. Or charity of Copts. How hot it must be on the roof for them, thought Porfiri. Evicted from *down there*, they lived nearer to the Father than to the Son.

An old nun with a cross tatooed on her forehead squatted to grind chickpeas. A monk and a nun together drew up a bucket from some well. Where does that water come from? Porfiri asked himself. Amiably strolling, with Joseph and his dragoman, the Novgorod amateur met two remembered lions, at the roof edge. Black plaits did their best to conceal the lions. Plaits of Isis, thought Porfiri. Ozoro Esther, surprised, watching the sunset.

PART 3

Communion
At Troitsky Cathedral, outside the hostel, all the half-saints. Strange to conduct a pilgrim army to Palestine. Their banners

didn't burn him. He'd have liked to lie in bed with the counter-pane up. All the puppets had brought their shrouds. Eyes stared only ahead. Porfiri felt shifty, it appeared he didn't have a ruling passion. Shifty but not penitent. Nikon considered *her* a penitent woman.

No communion today, he wanted to say to Filaret. They changed Christ into someone else. Everyone is agreeable, really. Beards, hats, disguises. Teeth. All that apparatus. The real Christ is *incommunicado*.

Filaret furiously censed. Saints and dead led the prayers of the congregation. Porfiri couldn't pronounce his dead family names. The Royal Door closed against him. He was cousinless, sisterless, among the dead. The Virgin of Vladimir, even the Virgin of the Bleeding Cheek, couldn't help. He couldn't offer incense to the pictures and to the people.

Evidence

Shuffling around town, he accused himself. Hatless, he amazed his passing charges. Smacked himself repeatedly. Reading, writing, arithmetic, a little sense. No geography, no Palestine. He addressed himself as someone far off. Who said Porfiri should come to Palestine? Maybe in a hermitage he'd have unwound himself. He thought of the Iconostasis. He cried. No no open the door.

Shuffleshoes around town till assailed by tattooists outside the Armenian Monastery. They were jabbing pilgrims with needles. A young charge was crying. It hurt to have the Savior worked into her arm. J E R U S A L E M also, and the year of *hajj*. Tattooists were calling out, Won't you have a *hajji?*

Won't you have a *hajji?* He brushed off the Arab tout. Not the right day for all that. Feet were going up the street forever. Porfiri. He stopped his shuffle. Porfiri Uspenski. Turning he raised his hand to punish this tout. He'd have punished the saffron scarf of Esther Ozoro. She was a tall mosque in the five o'clock light. If you don't have a *hajji*, Porfiri, no one in Russia will believe you're a pilgrim. Her attendant princesses didn't understand her Arabic, they stared hard at this hatless man. A great *moujik* who'd had learning poured over him, then shaken it off in one irritated movement.

Won't *you* have *a hajji?* Yes, I will. She took her saffron through the penitent women, and sat down in a tattoing booth. He sat down next to her. The tattooist picked up a needle. The usual Easter

Savior, I suppose? Oh no. Just J E R U S A L E M. And the year.
1853. She laid her arm on the table, then she made an unpopu-
lated place of the booth. A second tattooist worked on Porfiri's arm.
Dipped his needles into an ink of soot and red wine. Porfiri didn't
look at anyone either. They ignored her ladies, his charges, and
the loitering Armenian monks. Cowled curiosity. Town and year
worked into their skin, they rose, the princess paid with a Maria
Theresa dollar, he in rubles, they walked out through the crowd.

Catechism
Do you make the sign of the Cross with two fingers or three, Porfiri?
Two, Ozoro Esther. Unlike the Greeks.
Do you sing Alleluia three times or twice, Porfiri?
Twice, Ozoro Esther. Unlike the Greeks.
All the same, Porfiri, I doubt the entire legitimacy of your service.
I'm not the Pan-Slavic Messiah, Ozoro Esther.
I think the Orthodox Church could take itself a little
more in hand.
You're a great deal more severe than my friend the Patriarch.
The Ethiopian Patriarch isn't enriched with knowledge.
It seems you're angry I've come without a hat.
Hatless you are an embarrassment. What will you do, Porfiri? Trot
back to Filaret?
Tonight, perhaps, I'll sleep at the Armenians.
What do you feel on the subject of Constantinople, Porfiri? Do you
feel the Tsar will oblige?
Constantinople will be ours.
You look so hatless, Porfiri Uspenski. Won't you come with me? Do
you want to stay at the Armenian Hospice forever?

Cousins
A hurdy-gurdy in the Christian Quarter perhaps paid for someone's
pilgrimage. It imposed its repertoire under the chandelier where
they lay. The chandelier, that first cousin of the hurdy-gurdy. He
touched her tattooed arm. Black plaster still covered the town
and their year.
   Porfiri . . . How I hate all the P's. The Patriarch, your pilgrims,
my princesses. All the P's except you, Porfiri.
   On the chair her lions. They say they cannot guard the princess
now.

PART 4

Appointment
I'll meet you at Tecla Haimanat Convent. This afternoon.
What time this afternoon?
Three sharp on the needles.
Who's Tecla Haimanat, Esthalina? (Gentle, at three sharp on the needles.)

Tecla Haimanat
Tecla Haimanat waded into Hippopotamus Lake. He stood there, seven years in full canonicals, till his leg fell off. Seven years, a great brain. A hippopotamus carried his leg off to a healing shrine. But it's not his real one. That's just a leg in religion. The real leg, the real shinbone, the real second right toe, said goodbye to religion. You see that picture up there, Porfiri. There he is, waving it. He hits out at pagans with it, Danakil. He bangs with that leg at heaven. He does everything he can to go home.

Another
Tecla Haimanat waved his game leg at heaven. It looked like the transverse of a cross. Lake-brooder, darker than Danakil, tearer of maps drawn by accurate Europe.
   The Ethiopian Church turned over on its side, somberly laughed, went back to sleep.

Abuna
What was the Abuna like, Esthalina?
He lived to a memorandum pad. Once my mother sent me to him with a message. Ozoro Esther, he said, there are 2356 priests waiting outside to be ordained. I cannot give you more than an hour, my dear.

Butter
The ignorant ordinands scowled outside thinking of prayers, bogs, and women. The butter they anointed their hair with ran down them in the atheist sun. The map of Ethiopia streamed with that grease, it stained Gondar and Debre Tabor. The Lion of Judah sat down on a buttery throne. Sworded angels at his side couldn't stop the buttery contraband. It got into Ozoro Esther's eyes. Porfiri, she said, save me from all that religious butter.

Brondo

They'd lead an ox into the dining room. Actually, Porfiri, it was the ox that made it a dining room. It stared at us, it seemed about as big as Ethiopia. Brown as an Abuna. Into this big room, covered with Venetian glass. (Of course, all shattered, years back.) The cook would come over, I call him cook for your sake, Porfiri. What cut would you like, Ozoro Esther? I'd indicate it, the ox would stand there incredulous, stare at us, then that cook neatly carved my cut off its flank. Stare and howl. The cut would be served raw. All the finesse went into the carving. Cuts for the whole court. The Abuna blessed everyone. You could see the ox reflected in a hundred pieces of that Venetian glass. Afterward they'd made love under the table. Love was the second course. They call that meat *brondo,* Porfiri. Brondo is a great bone-builder.

Mariam Barea

Butter outside, brondo inside. My mother was a nasty woman. They called her the leper queen, she was afraid they were right. Bafana the leper. Her physician prescribed a cure of children. She had a basketful of their hands, the fetishist.

The buffoon Bafana, I said to my sisters. So she married me off to a man I didn't like. Mariam Barea, a very popular man. That's why I disliked him. But it was her mistake because I got to like him. He was the best soldier in Gondar, I think the best man. We lived half a year together.

She crossed out her mistake, he was charged with stealing land from the monks of Magwena. To make me a pleasure-garden. The monks went to the Abuna, the Abuna to Bafana, then he was excommunicated. Then they cut his throat. Like they cut a sheep's throat, Porfiri. The ox they kept alive.

PART 5

Gifts

A scent box hung over her bosom.
You're wearing a scarlet jacket today, Esthalina.
So the enemy can't see the wound he's inflicted, Porfiri.
Here's an Easter egg for you. Happy Easter, Esther Ozoro.

I have one for you also, Porfiri. Please smile. Someone pecked his way out of the shell.

Puppetry

Two play-acting friars, one Joseph of Arimathea the other Nicodemus, took down the feigned body from its Cross. They reverently disposed of the arms, then carried this puppet Christ from Cavalry to the Unction Stone. Porfiri's wood children looked on with great eyes.

On the Roof: Easter

Two little black kawasses clear a way. Crowns and crosses and umbrellas, all that gold. Under an umbrella, the Bishop. Here are the pilgrim princesses. Welletta Israel, Wezorah Amarg, Esther Ozoro the young widow. Bom. The Son, from a three-fingered banner, stares hard. But his Coptic Mother scowls. Bom, a big slow man says. Bom, and just in time to support a rhythm, Bom.

The Sermon

Bom. Someone exhorts them in Geez. (If only we understood Geez, they sigh. Bore us in Amharic, the language we took our lovers in. Worse than Nestorians those Copts? They can be Armenians for all we care.) Who gave the Coptic guardian that key? Bom. A ripeness leans against the shoulder of her sister. Kicks a slipper off. The Bishop, he has a sleepy way with a hand-cross. Let's retire under my burnoose. All the bored linen of the Abyssinian maids. They're settling down for the night in Deir-as-Sultan.

Candidates

In dream he was flying over the mummy-city. Who'll force the lid off? he cried. Candidate souls from the Sergievsky hostel held up their relics, he inspected them. A sackful of shrouds, a teapot, a candle.

Jaffa Gate

The town wall scared him. Going in, through Jaffa Gate, he seemed to himself an innocent priest from Novgorod, from All-Russia.

The time will come, Porfiri, you'll be scared to go through that gate.

Sitters pressed upon him to be identified: Joseph in his dwarfish; chair; Anba Basilius in his Coptic chair; *shish-bash* players, lollers. The town was full of churches and chairs. Joseph leans forward to inquire about the healing properties of black plaster; Filaret at table alludes spinningly to the Queen of the South. The sitter keeps his status quo. Porfiri runs.

The Photograph
Smile please said the Mission photographer. Porfiri and Esthalina stood among the cabbage-soup pilgrims. Porfiri was nearer to brondo than to bread, to Gondar than to Novgorod, to Esthalina than to himself. She was invisible. The photograph trap could not close on her. Maybe she was the town, and that was where he now stood, inside walls closed off from the climbing pilgrims.

S.S. *Goodbye*
Esthalina loves only early wheels. Hurry hurry she says or we'll be late.

They hear the last of town. Sisterly stirrings of a choir of dead bats. He bows ironically to the Wall and his sisters.

Esthalina's webbed in muslin against spies. The carriage wheels speak only American. At Jaffa the batcries meet them. Spiteful cries crossing the harbor. There the ship waits. The Fanny Skinner.

Palestine pilgrims, goodbye. Monks or worse, goodbye. We've locked our trunks against you.

The crew speak only American. Porfiri tries out new names. Malta, Gibraltar, the overland route. New York, he says flashingly, Esthalina. New York, Porfiri? Her plaits, democratic, in New York? All those harbor lights. Porfiri, I'll comb my hair for the town.

THREE POEMS

ROBERT DUNCAN

ACHILLES

I do not know more than the sea tells me,
told me long ago, or I overheard her
    telling distant roar upon the sands,
waves of meaning in the cradle of whose
    sounding and resounding power I
    slept.   Manchild, she sang,
or was it a storm uplifting the night
    into a moving wall in which
I was carried as if a mothering nest had
    been made in dread,

the wave of a life darker than my
    life before me sped, and I,
larger than I was, grown dark as
    the shoreless depth,
arose from myself shaking the last
    light of the Sun
from me.   Manchild, she said:

Come back to the shores of what you are.
Come back to the crumbling shores.
    All night
the mothering tides in which your
    life first formd in the brooding light
    have quencht the bloody splendors of the sun,
and under the triumphant processions
    of the moon lay down
thunder upon thunder of an old
    longing,   the beat

of whose repeated spell
        consumes you.
                    Thetis then,
my mother, has promised me
the mirage of a boat, a vehicle
    of water within the water,
and my soul would return from
    the trials of its human state,
from the long siege, from the
    struggling companions upon the plain,
from the burning towers and deeds
    of honor and dishonor,
the deeper unsatisfied war beneath
    and behind the declared war,
and the rubble of beautiful, patiently
    workt moonstones, agates, jades,
            obsidians,
turnd and returnd in the wash of
    the tides, the gleaming waste,
the pathetic wonder,

words turnd in the phrases of song
    before our song, or are they . . . ?

                    beautiful
    patiently workt remembrances of those
        long gone from me,
returnd anew, ghostly in the light
    of the moon, old faces.

For Thetis, my mother, has promised
    me a boat,
a lover, an up-lifter of my spirit
into the rage of my first element
    rising, a Princedom
in the Unreal, a share in Death.

Time, time, it's time.
The business of Troy has long been done.
Achilles in Leuke has come home.
And soon you too
      will be alone.

A GLIMPSE

    Come yellow broom
and lavender in bloom,
the path runs down to the shady stream,

yet by your magic and the loud bees'
    hum,
      perfume of sage and lavender in bloom,

hot and dreaming in the morning sun
I ever from where I am return
as if from this boyhood privacy
my life burnd on in a smoke of me

mixt with sage in the summer air,
    and lavender,
and the stream from its shade
runs down to the bay and beyond to the sea.

ANCIENT QUESTIONS

Art thou brooding, Old Man, upon thy works?
staring in gloomy depths where
                incubate thy deeds?
Not with these seeds of discontent began
    the curse that Earth's dark agents
    sow in the dreams of Man,
Not with these Cantos first we heard
    where the ancient contest twixt
    good and evil consequences ran.

And who has loosend the bonds of that snare?
Our spirits strive against whose toils?
In the first light after dawn, whose
    Boys, crying loud to one another,
entangle the little birds in nets of
    cunning Art? whose messengers
bring, already, news, alas, that
    moves the heart against its will?
What instigator hid among these notes
    painful harmonies in the song we sing?
What adversary brings our words to harry us,
    ringing in our ears when we'd be still?

                    ✸

        Job, Iyyôb, the enemy, enmity and righteousness in one,
ôyeb, inveterate foe of Him he obeys, cries out: "Yahwe
gave and took away. Blessed be His Name in what He does."
He tore his robe and shaved his head. The starry legions
groand in his shame.
        You think I have but read this story? Or that I have
put aside from my thought the despairing Poet's face? His
eyes stare into the shadows where the hostile flight of
demonic wings shows and vanishes, a flicker out of fire
returning like rime the ominous after-intentions of the Word
shows Father to the thought. "I alone escaped to tell you,"
each messenger relates: "The rest are dead or dying. The
walls of your story have falln away."

The name may be explaind by the Arabic root *wb*, "return,
repent." Rome in all its rimes remains, advances into ruin;
and the scholar explains that, back of Iyyôb, the prince of
Ashtorth in Bashan bears the name Ayyab, an older form of
the same, from the Akkadian Ayya– abu(m), "Where is (My)
Father?"

The Elohim brooding upon these Waters are appalld.

And you could recant, Old Man, recall?
Look deep into your sight and you will find
a deeper blindness where you were
                    stricken blind,
our own, revision of the Truth we see
the Poet stumbles upon.   Beauty
alone triumphant in the light of noon
turns back the Day upon itself
embittered, and Night bereft of dreams
is like a deserted railway station
after hours or in an age of inanition.
Will the last train never come? Come?
Or has it gone and left us? Old . . .

And you do not think the Day and the Night
     can speak?
He overhears their curses and embittering words.

The Silence does not put my heart to rest
     but works me up, works me up.
As if in Emptiness there were infant echoes
     crying,   and Death
refuses me.   Whom God has fenced about.
          Whose Way is hidden from him.

He yearns:

"Now a word came to me quietly,
"Just a whisper caught my ear.
"In a nightmare, in a trance,
"When other men are sleeping,
"A breath passt over my face,
"The hair of my body bristled,
"I was transfixt, held down where I was,
"my heart beating under the weight of it."

"Paused, but I could not see who it was.
"Just a shadow before my eyes.
"A hush, then I heard a voice saying:
" 'Twixt morning and evening they are shattered.
  'They perish forever nameless . . .' "

The scholar comments: "Zophar is sure that God must have
something against Job and could make it known if he
cared to speak of it."

And didst thou ride the Wind, Old Man?
high in the roar of the promised year?
And in your verses scan immortal voices
thundering certainties? Love and Light
            rain down
from clouds in which the spirit ran?
The wind dies and moans among its leavings,
ways of desolation workt
            among the works of men.

THE MOONLIGHT SONATA

YANNIS RITSOS

Translated from the Greek by Rae Dalven

TRANSLATOR'S NOTE: *Yannis Ritsos was born in Monemvasia, in the Peloponnesos, Greece, in May, 1909, and began to write poetry when he was eight years old. He graduated from the High School of Gytheio and went to Athens to continue his studies, but at seventeen he became seriously ill and was subsequently hospitalized for long stretches of time in several sanatoria. Yet despite a history of tuberculosis, Ritsos is one of Greece's most prolific and widely published poets.*

Ritsos' poetry, which first appeared in the Large Greek Encyclopedia (Pyrsos) *when he was eighteen, includes more than thirty books published over a span of forty years. His work may be divided into four periods, the last of which Ritsos himself likes to think of as his "Fourth Dimension." In his formative period of the early 1930's, we find in such works as* Tractor (1934), Pyramids (1935), Epitaph (1936), *poems that integrate the poet's personal, social and ideological experiences. In his second period, covering the fervent years of the late 1930's he produced* Song of My Sister (1937) *and* Spring Symphony (1938), *excerpts from which have appeared in English, translated by Rae Dalven (*Modern Greek Poetry, *1950, Gaer Associates), and* March of the Ocean (1940). *In all of these, Ritsos blends lyricism, simplicity of language, and unusual pictorial and dramatic sensitivity to sustain the social consciousness which is at the basis of all his work and serves to iden-*

167

tify it. His third period covers the Nazi occupation, the civil war and his years of exile that followed. Trial (1943), Our Comrade (1945), The Man with the Carnation (1952), Sleeplessness (1954) are some of the works which belong to this period.

The Moonlight Sonata (1956), for which Ritsos won the National Poetry Prize of Greece, certainly belongs to his mature "Fourth Dimension." The poems of this period manifest a synthesis of his mature social philosophy, both subjective and objective, expressed with his characteristic lyricism and simplicity of language. Other outstanding recent works are Farewell (1957), Chronicle (1957), When the Stranger Comes (1958), The Window (1960), The Bridge (1960) and Beneath the Shadow of the Mountain (1962).

Ritsos' poetry has been translated into fourteen European languages, and anthologies of his work have been brought out in Russian, Rumanian, Czech and German. Four of his long poems, translated into French by D. Beraha and A. Kataza, appear in Quatrième Dimension (Pierre Seghers, 1958). His epic poem Romiossini is now available in English, translated by O. Laos (Dustbooks, 1969), in addition to his Selected Poems (Smyrna Press, 1969) and the Poems of Yannis Ritsos, translated by Alan Page (the Review, no. 21, June–October, 1969). Several of Ritsos' shorter poems have been set to music by Mikos Theodarakis.

Exiled more than once for his progressive ideas, Ritsos was forced to spend the years from 1948 to 1952 in Lemnos, Macronisos and St. Strati. In April 1967, on the day the present Greek military junta took over, he was removed from his home in Athens at 5:00 A.M. and exiled to Leros, where he was incarcerated for the next sixteen months. Because of illness, Ritsos was released in the summer of 1968 and hospitalized. He now resides in Samos with his wife and young daughter, seriously weakened by his many years in exile and his chronic tubercular condition.—R.D.

A spring night. A large room in an old house. An old woman dressed in black is speaking to a young man. They have not turned on the light. A relentless moonlight streams in through the two windows. I forgot to say that the Woman in Black has published two or three interesting collections of poetry of a religious nature. So, the Woman in Black is speaking to the Young Man:

Let me come along with you. What a moon tonight!
It is a fine moon,—my hair will not show
that it has grown white. The moon
will turn my hair once more into gold. You will not
     be able to notice.
Let me come along with you.

When there is a moon the shadows in the house grow larger,
invisible hands draw the curtains aside,
a pallid finger writes forgotten words on the dust
of the piano—I do not want to hear them. Be still.

Let me come along with you.
A little farther down, as far as the brickyard enclosure,
down to the place where the road bends and the city
appears cemented and airy, whitewashed with moonlight
so indifferent and immaterial
as positive as metaphysics
so that you can finally believe that you exist and that you
     do not exist
that you have never existed, that time and its ruin
     have not existed
Let me come along with you.

              •   •   •

We will sit down for a bit on the stone bench,
     on that elevation
and as the spring breeze blows on us
we can even imagine that we will fly,
because, quite often, and even now, I can hear the noise
     of my dress
like the noise of two powerful wings flapping open and shut,
and when you lock yourself within this sound of the flight
you feel your neck tightened, your sides, your flesh,
and so, squeezed inside the muscles of the sky-blue air,
within the robust nerves of the elevation,

it does not matter whether you go or whether you return
nor does it matter that my hair has grown white,
(this is not my sorrow—my sorrow
is that my heart does not also grow white).
Let me come along with you.

I know that every human being journeys alone toward love,
alone toward glory and alone toward death.
I know it. I have tried it. It is useless.
Let me come along with you.

This house has become haunted, it drives me away—
I mean to say that it is very old, the nails are loosening,
the picture frames fall as if they are plunging into the void,
the pieces of plaster fall noiselessly
as the hat of the dead man falls off the clothes hanger
            in the dreary hallway
as the frayed woolen glove of silence falls from her lap
or as a ribbon of moonlight falls on the old
            disemboweled armchair.

·   ·   ·

There was a time when it too was young,—not the photograph
            you're looking at in such disbelief—
I am speaking of the armchair, so comfortable, you could sit
            in it for hours on end
and with eyes shut you could dream of any chance thing whatever
—a stretch of sandy beach, dampened, polished by the moon,
more highly polished than my old patent leather shoes that I
            give once a month to the corner shoeshine stand,
or a sail of a fishing boat disappearing in the deep,
            cradle-rocked by its very own breath,
a triangular sail folded like a handkerchief, diagonally,
            only in two,
as if it had nothing to enclose in it or to keep
or to wave open-wide as a sign of farewell. I have always
            had a mania for handkerchiefs

not to keep anything tied in them,
any flower seeds or camomile gathered in the fields at sundown
or to tie them into four knots like the cap that the workers
      are wearing in the scaffolding opposite
or to wipe my eyes,—I have taken good care of my eyesight;
I have never worn glasses. Handkerchiefs are simply
      an eccentricity.

Now I fold them in four, in eight, in sixteen
to give my fingers something to do. And now I remember
that this is how I measured music when I attended
      the conservatory
with a blue apron on and a white collar, with two
      blonde braids—8, 16, 32, 64,—
held by the hand of a little peach tree friend of mine,
      all light and rose flowers,
(forgive these words of mine—a bad habit)—32, 64,—and my
      people had sustained
high hopes in my musical talent. Well then, I was telling you
      about the armchair—
disemboweled—the rusty springs, the straw can be seen—
I thought I would take it next door to the cabinetmaker,
but where is the time, the money and the inclination—
      what can you repair first?
I was thinking of throwing a sheet over it,—I was afraid
of the white sheet in such a moonlight. Here sat people
who dreamed big dreams, as you and especially as I dreamed,
and now they repose beneath the earth without being bothered
      by the rain or the moon.
Let me come along with you.

We will stop a little at the head of the marble stairway
      of St. Nicholas
afterward you will walk down the stairs and I will turn back
with the warmth of the chance touch of your jacket on my left,
and also several square-shaped lights from the small
      neighborhood windows
and this very white mist from the moon that looks like a long
      procession of silvery swans—

and I am not afraid of this expression, for at one time,
on many spring nights I used to converse with God who appeared
        before me
robed in the mist and the glory of such a moonlight,
and I sacrificed to him many young men, even handsomer than you
so white and inaccessible to vaporize myself in my white flame,
        in the whiteness of the moonlight.
inflamed by the ravenous eyes of men and the indecisive ecstasy
        of the adolescents
besieged by exquisite, sun-tanned bodies,
vigorous limbs developed at swimming, at rowing,
        on the race track, at football (that I pretended not to see)
brows, lips and necks, knees, fingers and eyes,
chests, arms and thighs (and I really did not see them)
—you know, sometimes, admiring, you forget what it is
        you admire, your admiration is enough for you.—
My God, what star-studded eyes, and I kept lifting myself
        in an apotheosis of negated stars
because, besieged in this way from without and from within,
no other road was left me except going uphill
        or going downhill.—
                No, it is not enough.
Let me come along with you.

I know that now it is way past the hour. Do let me,
because for so many years, days and nights and purple afternoons,
        I have been alone,
unyielding, alone and immaculate,
even in my conjugal bed immaculate and alone,
composing glorious verses on the knees of God,
verses that, I assure you, will remain like sculptures
        on unblemished marble
beyond my life and your life, way beyond. It is not enough.
Let me come along with you.

            •   •   •

This house no longer gives me a lift.
I can no longer endure to carry it on my back.
You always have to be careful, be careful
to support the wall with the large buffet
to support the buffet with the very antique carved table
to support the table with the chairs
to support the chairs with your hands
to put your shoulder under the rafter that is about to give way.
And the piano, like a black closed coffin. You do not dare
      open it.
Always to be careful, to be careful that they do not fall, that
      you do not fall, I cannot bear it.
Let me come along with you.

This house, despite all of its dead people, has no intention
      of dying.
It persists on living with its dead,
living off its dead
living on the assurance of its own death
and even housing its dead on dilapidated beds and shelves.
Let me come along with you.

Here, no matter how softly I may walk in the evening mist,
either in my slippers, or barefoot,
something will creak,—a windowpane cracks or some mirror,
some footsteps are heard,—they are not my own.
Outside, on the street, perhaps these footsteps are not heard,—
repentance, they say, wears wooden sabots,—
and if you attempt to look at this or the other mirror,
behind the dust and the cracks,
you perceive that your face is more indistinct
      and more lacerated,
your face for which you asked no other thing of life
      except to keep it clean and indivisible.

The lips of the drinking glass sparkle in the moonlight
like a circular razor—how can I bring it up to my lips?
Much as I may thirst,—how can I bring it? Do you see?
I still have an inclination for making comparisons,—this has
      stayed with me,

this is what still gives me the assurance that I am not away.
Let me come along with you.

From time to time, during the hour of twilight, I have
         the feeling
that outside the windows the bear trainer is passing by
         with his very aged, plodding bear
with her wool all thorns and thistles
raising the dust on the neighborhood road
a desolate cloud of dust incensing the twilight
and the children have returned to their homes for dinner
         and they do not let them go out again
although behind the walls they can make out the footsteps
         of the aged bear—
and the bear, wearied, marches within the wisdom
    '   of her loneliness, not knowing where to and why—
she has grown heavy, she can no longer dance on her hind legs
she can no longer wear her little lace cap to entertain
         the children, the unemployed, the fastidious,
and the only thing she wants is to lie down on the earth,
allowing them to step on her belly freely, playing her final
         game in this fashion,
manifesting her terrifying strength for renunciation,
her heedlessness of the interests of others, the rings
         on her lips, the needs of her teeth,
her heedlessness of pain and of life
with the certain alliance of death—even of a slow death—
her ultimate heedlessness of death with the continuance and the
         knowledge of life
that rises with understanding and activity above her slavery.

But who can continue to play this game to the very end?
And the bear lifts herself once more and resumes her journey
submitting to her leash, her rings, her teeth,
smiling with her lacerated lips at the nickles and dimes that
         the handsome and unsuspecting children throw at her
(handsome precisely because they are unsuspecting)
and saying thank you. For the only thing that bears
that have aged have learned to say is: thank you, thank you.
Let me come along with you.

This house is suffocating. Indeed the kitchen
is like the bottom of the sea. The coffee pots hanging
        on the walls glisten
like the round, large eyes of improbable fish,
the plates sway slowly like medusas,
seaweeds and seashells are entangled in my hair—later I cannot
        pull them out,
I cannot rise again to the surface—
the tray falls noiselessly from my hands,—I collapse
and I see the air bubbles of my breath rising, rising—
and seeing them I try to amuse myself
and I ask myself what would one who finds himself above
        and sees these air bubbles say,
would he perhaps think that someone is drowning, or that a diver
        is probing the depths of the sea?

And honestly, it isn't only a few times that I have discovered
        there at the sinking-bottom
corals and pearls and treasures of shipwrecked vessels,
improvised meetings, of yesterday and today and the future,
almost a confirmation of eternity,
a certain catching of the breath, a certain smile
        of immortality, as they say,
a good fortune, an intoxication, and even enthusiasm,
corals and pearls and sapphires;
only that I do not know how to give them—no I do give them;
only that I do not know if they can accept them—in any case
        I give them.
Let me come along with you.

One moment, so I may get my jacket.
In this inconstant weather, however slight, we must take care
        of ourselves.
The evenings are humid and the moon
does it not seem to you, really, that it intensifies the chill?
Let me button up your shirt—how powerful your chest is,
how powerful the moon,—the armchair, I say,—and when I lift
        the cup from the table
a hole of silence is left underneath, I immediately place
        my palm over it

so that I may not look into it,—I set the cup down again
        in its place;
and the moon a hole in the cranium of the world—do not look
        in there,
there is a magnetic power that pulls you toward it—do not look,
        do not look there,
listen to me who is speaking to you—you will fall in.
        This vertigo
beautiful, weightless,—you will fall,—
the moon is a marble well,
shadows move and mute wings, mysterious voices—don't you
        hear them?
Deep—deep the fall,
deep—deep the ascent,
the ethereal statue steady in its outspread wings
deep—deep the inexorable benefaction of silence,—
quavering illuminations of the other shore, as you oscillate
        in your own wave,
a breath of ocean. Beautiful, weightless,
is this vertigo,—be careful, you will fall. Do not look at me,
for me my place is oscillation—the superb vertigo. It is like
        this every evening
I have a slight headache, a kind of dizziness.

.   .   .

Often I run over to the drugstore opposite to get some aspirin,
that at other times I am lazy and I remain with my headache,
to listen to the hollow noise made by the water pipes inside
        the walls,
or I brew a cup of coffee, and, forever preoccupied,
I forget myself and I prepare two—who is going to drink
        the other cup?—
It is really amusing, I let it get cold on the window sill
or sometimes I drink the second cup too as I look out
        the window at the green lamp of the drugstore,
like the green light of a noiseless train coming to carry me off
with my handkerchiefs, my shoes down at the heels, my black rag,
        my poems,

without a single valise—what can you do with them?
Let me come along with you.

Ah, are you leaving? Good night. No, I am not coming.
          Good night.
I shall go out in a little while. Thank you. Because,
          after all,
I must leave this broken-down house.
I must see something of the city,—no, not the moon—
the city with her callused hands, the city of the wage earner
the city that swears in the name of bread and in the name
          of its fist
the city that carries all of us on her back
with our pettinesses, our vices, our animosities
with our aspirations, our ignorance and our agedness,—
so I may hear the large strides of the city,
no longer to hear your footsteps
nor the footsteps of God, nor my own footsteps. Good night.

*The room is darkened. It seems that some cloud must have hidden
the moon. Suddenly, as if a hand had increased the volume of the
radio in the neighborhood bar, a very familiar musical phrase was
heard. And then I understood that "The Moonlight Sonata" accompanied in a low voice only the first part of that whole scene.
Now the Young Man will be going down the slope with an ironical
and perhaps a compassionate smile on his well-shaped lips and with
a feeling of freedom. When he arrives precisely at St. Nicholas
Church, before he goes down the marble stairway, he will laugh, a
loud laugh, irrepressible. His laughter will not sound discordant
beneath the moon. Perhaps the only thing discordant is that it is not
at all discordant. Soon after the Young Man will become silent, he
will become serious and say: "The decadence of an epoch." Thus
completely calm once more, he will again unbutton his shirt and
take to the road. As for the Woman in Black, I do not know if she
finally came out of her house. The moonlight shines again. And
in the corners of the room the shadows are squeezed together by
an unbearable repentance, almost anger, not so much at life, as
at the uselessness of confession. Do you hear? The radio continues:*

SEVEN POEMS

YUKI HARTMAN

The man was looking. Inside his
Flesh with the tools too sharp,
I was scared but looked in
Too, holding onto his strong rib.

He was moving, there, like the valve
With a warning system, warning me
In the bones and I fell from the rib,
I saw nothing. And I forced myself

With tools too soft. They all fell
Down, leaving their hands on the rib
That dangled so nonchalantly that
Sun was coming out like the water.

The medium height of my lemon tree,
Holds the citrus water in the bag
Of yellow oiled lamb in the belly—
the forks he spread or the long leg

Under the grave to strike the new
Deep, nudging the black soil under
Water to jump up to kiss the tree—
Here, my tree sipped the new water.

I was drowning. Asleep. The streaks of
Blue were separating the
Shoulder blades from the small neck,
The steel tree growing in my stomach.

Oh, I had the colors in the meanwhile,
Pulping out the sour taste
On the floor where my bed was dug.
Father, with a stiff branch, admonished me.

I kept sleeping. Thinking how lovely it is
To be drowning, where
I heard the sharp clutter at the front gate
And Father struggling with Death to wake me.

Slowly, too, to turn the glass
Eye in the music box you tanned
On the oven and munching the corners
Humming a Schubert song so haltingly.

The fan, too, slowly turning up
Side down on the monologue you
Made up in your concert of roses
Grown in the bush of my blueness.

Slowly, slowly, your falling eye
In the sun or the blue flesh I
Open in the blood; and you see
I am your son growing like you.

The letters leaping like something like love,
Stamped on the hood and so restless inside
A telephone call from the underground water,
Potentially to be extracted from the skins

Of love. Opened and read. Read and closed
Secretly in the head to stomp again, I feel
Rapt as I read, the rumbling pulses, still
Caressing in the papers and daydreaming so,

Under the letters were hands of friendship,
The papers that are not letters at all,
As always, these sweet passages recalling,
I say, "adieu," and I want to thank you all.

Like the iris, growing in the shrubbery on the estate
Where no sun soaked, the flood was like the bloody sun
All at once, is over, the bright sand fell. The shady
Shrubbery bled not at all, was dark in the afternoon.

And when *that* was swept aside, like the old ceremonies,
The sun as innocent as before was traveling up around
On the horizon where herons were seen carrying something
Uncanny: Perhaps it was the bundle of babies for elders,

Or it was something extracted from the sun, the medicine
For the extinction. The younger hunters hooked the herons
All over the estate and at evenings, when it was quiet,
Stepped in the shrubbery, and found the iris not at all.

This boy to ripple through the water,
Finding the girls with the golden tail,
The bodies that separate the blue walls
In the ocean where he lies with a grip

On the spear. They go like the fish
Around the walls and tops of the sunken
Ship, where he sees the familiar swish
Of the shark in the mess hall corridor.

And his skull was blue also, the slow
Progress of his dreams under the water
Broke, long ago, and he stared lightly
Blue water going through his blue groin.

JOSEPHINE'S LITERARY CHOICE

MARVIN COHEN

I

A student of contemporary literary criticism had stopped living some time ago, and had been reading instead. Like a swarm of locusts devouring a dry California plateau, she'd work her way through the *quality* contents of one branch library after another. The resources of her means of private finance were too slender to permit her to own so many books herself; but the central library and the university library, unlike branch libraries, were continually replenished and amply inexhaustible. Her goal, plodding through book after book, was to develop her critical and interpretive faculties and to apply them to every serious book ever written since the ancient discovery of words: but employing the sharp instruments of modern ways of evaluating all the dateless literary material. The most advanced standards were hers; she was thirty years old and wore glasses, had never been married, but caught the eye of the beholder as being uncommonly pretty when looked at one way; or average passable when scrutinied the other. The "point of view" reveals the character.

Here it was, another Saturday evening, in the reading room of the almost oppressively omnipotent central library. She was being thirty years old and undated by any man that night; rather, all her gentleman escorts were the *authors* she was reading; almost all of whom were past their virile prime, being dead. It's hard to have a *personal* relationship with even a *handsome* dead man; even though he had been lionized, like the thrilling Lord Byron.

She stopped ruminating along literary lines long enough to take pause, sum up, take stock, and begin worrying: would she ever be a wife and mother? If so, she must hurry. Her prime was not getting riper. She had poured love into literature, as payment to purchase the art of mastering its scale of values for the purposes of being a connoisseur critic. But she had neglected her role as a *woman*. It wasn't too late. The alarm had been on time.

The warning is throbbing in her body. She must soon be mated. The right man would have to be found. She'd apply her hyper-literary taste to the more earthly plane of men, to choose indeed a worthy lover as the proper fit for her pride. She would not be sold short. A demigod would suit her fine, equal as a man to Dante, Goethe, or Cervantes as towering makers of word worlds. Her standards might be too exacting; but having laboriously acquired them, in painstaking remittance of toil, she was loath to lower them. She listed specifications that her prospective man would have to meet; should he fail them, he must be disqualified: just as certain authors—like Galsworthy, Maugham, Sinclair Lewis, E. E. Cummings, and Longfellow—simply didn't muster up. She had refined herself, and now at her just estimate and frank esteem, had no business to traffic with mediocrities in the literary realm or in her personal life. The test of character was to *enforce* the excellence of her acquired taste. As she spurned many authors as being comparatively unworthy, so, as a woman, she must do much rejecting before the right man became acceptable as her life's partner. She would exercise a rigor, in weeding out the candidates. Literature had taught her to be nobly exclusive—that is, excluding. She had perched a mentally lofty world for herself, which forbade most things to belong. Those that passed the test of belonging would *necessarily* have much to recommend them.

Great books were easily accessible, thanks to cheap modern type. But ranking *men* would have been snapped up and married by now, if they had the goods. On this score, she fell a-brooding, while Saturday night pounded away on the vast tables, stacked with opulent tomes, of the central library's hushed and velvety reading room.

Madame Bovary picked men from the romantic stereotype of books, and died in that martyrly cause. That example must be avoided. It would be stupid to parallel the good men to the good book. The standards were dissimilar; the *present* heroine of life, brooding late in the library, must recognize what a blunder it would be to equate the likely man with the masterful tome. She wouldn't beguile herself into the enchantment of a romantic trap on a literary basis, but would develop new criteria to separate men from literature, and by telling them apart, give both their full due of justice. This much was resolved. How to put it to practice, and to unbook herself of sentiments and notions of fancy and intellect peculiar to the bookish sphere of fictions and poetry, of drama and the essay; and to look full square at men, for what they are, divorced from the literary appraisal. This difficult transition, a phasing out from one quarter and an introduction to the other, needs be undergone, and now. Not a *translation* of one world by another; but learning a specifically different treatment. Such was her task. Thirty was a critical age. It prescribed recourses, however rash and desperate. The mastery of a new sphere of endeavor, like the learning of a new language, required submission to unfamiliar rules and an as yet foreign vocabulary; and a trial by new grammar.

What had happened to her as a girl from age fifteen to age thirty? Hadn't she put those years to *some* feminine account? Sure, so she wouldn't be starting from scratch, now. But how blinking novel is this outlook: like a mole that unburrows itself, startled by its first glare of the powerful sun, taken aback by rays so strangely un-underground. She must emerge from books, and be exposed to the rich torpor of sun and men. She'd rise into a woman's life: the more intense, for the background crawled up from. She'd be liberated *for* men, not *from* books. Not to *sacrifice* the latter; but to extol the former, as well.

From books, to graduate to men: from men, to *one* man: thus plotted her destiny, as closing time loomed up in the library's reading room. Her books in a pile before her, or strewn on the table in neglected stages of openness, spine up or spine down. She had thought through books, and her conclusion could be called "man." Her body had its biology to do; her heart needed companionship. She had done all that reading. She was mentally crammed with books. She was jammed with strategies of critical techniques for clustering the categories of books by their numerous cross-segmented designations; she was like Borges, or T. S. Eliot, or Dr. Johnson, in her extensive acquaintance with bodies of literature. Now, it was *life's* turn. When had she last had a *real* boyfriend? That was many books ago. She had measured out her life— in bookmarks! Now, the *woman* in her had put in a bid. An essential, basic demand by her own self-rooted cause. She would give it a womanly answer, by cramming it with man.

II

Scholars made their way out of the library. Josephine among them. She lightly trod toward her new life.

Having begun her dangerous decade of her thirties, she had almost belatedly managed to arm herself with her woman's destiny. Before which man should she dangle such a prize? Or where were there *any* men?

Her buoyancy became ponderous. It's nine o'clock of a Saturday night in the world's most colossal city, in winter's season of parties. She closed herself into a public telephone book, took out her notebook of phone numbers from her handbag that dangled from a shoulder strap, and with enough suitable coins at hand, began making a series of enquiries. One would be bound to work. A stray girl was always in demand.

On her fourth phone call, she connected with the right friends. They were a married couple, they were just off to a party, barely to the door before the phone call. They were so well invited, that it would be no problem for Josephine to accompany them. They gave her the party's address, and would meet her in front of the building, or in the lobby near the elevator. They'd get there before her, so Josephine should hurry and take a subway. A night of adventure were beginning to dawn. The future had unknown possibilities. It was close at hand. The party would be big, informal. No more delay by weighing what intriguingly lies before. Get down there, quick.

Bookish Josephine was riding on the subway. Could she read her way out into life, as she had read herself deep into books? Or would it make an awkward conversion—no, not conversion, but addition?

She wouldn't renounce books. She'd develop the woman side of her, and continue to read.

Her life was undergoing an extension: not relinquishing her cultivated sharp critical touch in giving books their qualities; *keeping* that, but venturing out into a love life, as well. Could her system accommodate both? Why not?—they weren't mutually antagonistic: neither excluded either; they were nonprohibitive pursuits. They would be tethered together, in a joint enterprise.

III

The party was going on. A youngish university professor, bourbon glass held high in hand, with whisky bubbles popping out when he shook his wiry arm in intensity, had Josephine engaged in a topic not unfamiliar to her: books. The vigor of their exchanges gave a frothy *brio* of high heady dash to their well-shared conversation. In a minute, he looked ready to propose. They were falling down a deep, mutual, headlong tunnel. Their animation was diving swoon-deep, and their plunge would reach a pit of bed. They were a naturally amorous pair.

All the party guests who came as couples, remained so. All the ones who came singly, had now paired off. Especially Josephine, and her professor. They were sitting together deep back on a couch, with their persons in frank, unfurtive contact, from foot to head, all up and down his whole left side, and her right side. Alcohol made their period of being strangers exquisitely brief. Barely introduced, they were now half intimate. This was progress! The library meditation was bearing an instant fruition, practically. Visions of sex united them in anticipatory frenzy. They emitted pants, in unison.

What an easy non-transition, from being totally lonely, to being divinely merged! Suddenly, and complete.

Absolutely they made one. It was happening. It was foregone; and denial vanished, aghast!

Total romantic fusion. Each one had forgotten himself, in the willing loss that meant surrender to a whole—by which they were so snugly bound, into which they thrust their all. Had love any lower definition? Or had love higher to go? No, they and love made a trio. And the warbling had no end.

But suddenly she snapped to. Her individualism asserted itself. She was Josephine, not part of anything.

"Who are you? I don't even know your name."

"I told you before, but you were inattentive with bliss: I'm Bob. Is that an obstacle to our marriage?"

"Why precipitantly do you bring up such a premature subject? We've erected no foundation as yet, to make that an inevitable step. Being baseless, you soar off to heights, expecting me to accompany you on your flights of caprice, your drunken romantic whimsy sodden with lust. Come down, and quick! Your nerve is all presumption, headstrong, impetuous, unfounded. You expect my timing to coincide with your gliding? Come down, right now! First learn of me, before you take liberties!"

IV

This chastening brought Bob up abruptly, and sobered him outright. How could she have spoiled it? It had been happening there between them; and then not! She had willfully halted it, in its immense stride. It had been sweeping them away, by momentum's full flight, to which they were held submissive as captives to the same happiness, together bound in one linked ecstasy. Now, she had shattered it! They had fallen into self-conscious parts. They were agonizingly separate. Overhead, and in front of them, the party blared forth. The other guests were now distinguished, that were a blur before. The couch they sat on was now their *arbitrary* link. What was nature's, now belonged to artifice. This sour wakening. By Josephine's sheer act of will. To prove her problematic freedom? To plunder the selfness of choice? By what law had she uglified their meeting into pure embarrassment bred by misadventure? In what strenuous perversity had she chanced to overcome a glorious rarity and undo a blessed accident? An uncommon destruction. To destroy an uncommon thing. Was too good a thing, too quickly come by, intolerable to her? Was bliss, by very intensity, unbearable as an utter stranger that had to be denied on impact? Bob wouldn't give up. He'd set Josephine the obligation of systematic explanation to account for her dastardly breaking of confidence and her rash conversion of doubly-bent innocence to the twin abyss of chasmic disaster on the ism of schism. He set an imperative on her apology. They would thrash this out, in a torture session. She wouldn't be let off lightly. She had provoked his devil, who would not be put off with appeasement. There would be thunder to pay. Josephine had provided an ordeal for herself; and Bob would vindictively hold her to it, till spasms of atonement come forth, and penance by mortification exacted. She toyed with a big thing, till it came apart; it would have to be paid for. She had to answer for what she destroyed. Bob packed her up in all her wintry effects and vehemently took his prisoner home: his, not hers. He'd drag insight from her captivity, and extract the most tortured confession. He'd bleed from her, book by book, all her drops of precious book-blood—it had to be shed. He'd drain her pale, look at the dregs, and tear from her his foremost conclusion on terms of white revenge, though her fainting might give a lethal signal in a white overspending of vitality's weakening reserve. Murder is meek, compared to what this murderer had done—she had murdered what was more precious than her bare self. Now her crime would be summoned, on their private trial. Only a personal justice can comply to a torn intimacy. What Bob was owed, was Josephine's to give.

V

They read book after book together. All was sweet restored harmony; she had in fact moved out of her own apartment and was living in his: well installed, along with his voluminous library. It was now the Easter vacation week away from university, so Bob's professional duties were relaxed and his devotion aided Josephine, whose studies had proliferated. She read at an alarming rate, and was far ahead of Bob who, for all his academic worth and his laureled prestige as a scholar, was no equal to Josephine's self-propelled genius. His ego was in conflict over this. As Josephine's lover, he had his pride to uphold. But he was easily outdistanced by her rapid consumption of books, which seemed like the progress of a disease: tuberculosis or some other wasting virus. Bob couldn't *catch up* with her; so the trick became, to slow her down.

How would she take his proposed rationing of her reading? Monomaniacally unwell.

"You won't interfere," she dictated. "We'll stop reading books together. I'll have my *own* reading life, independent of yours, and we'll each progress at rates apart, the way different trees or flowers do. Love is enough to share; love's principality is our meeting ground, and books would be redundant to it. We've joined our lives; but at this toll of compromise: let our minds have separate paths of development, as certainly mine does require. For you to entwine your restrictive ivy vine around my own advancing stem, to choke off its free growth and constrict my ever-promised flowering, would be the lover's crime that not even a court of love could condone. So let my mind go off, alone. Otherwise, I'll threaten to move out, and reluctantly add my *physical* independence to my insisted intellectual one. You won't head me off, for nature is determined in my high critical development; I'm beginning to write, and will produce major works to prove it. Don't let our emotions strangle my private mind. Set your pride aside, to grant me superior access, on a fertile field of solitude. Don't deny me this absolute, insisted condition; and the prize for your lenience, your side of the bargain, will be: you'll have me for a bride. Yet, don't construe this a bribe. Rejoice in my vaunted promise, and of your free joy, gladly give me pass; join, thus, your will to mine. And you'll be a major critic's husband. And I'll be: a dull professor's wife. If you're agreed, let's kiss and do more: and disrobe. We'll have a bouncing bed for our common ground; while my larger brain will do its divine hunting, remote from your smaller-sized one. Respect this division, not as an insult, but as nature's rugged and uneven law. Where there's no equality, I'll romp, while you'll slide. Show your big-souled acceptance of your lesser role, and nobly endure it. *I'm* the family's prodigy; while your level must hold on evenly to its mediocre allotment. This is not intended, but observed; and for our better life together, to be obeyed. Now, let's make love: just to prove that you're not *entirely* emasculated. Pardon my ascendency, in our natural comparison. In return, I'll grant you superior *masculinity*. Prove it, and pin me down, please."

VI

They were married in the marrying month of June. Bob let her live her own life, and took revenge, for being slighted, by sporadic infidelities with some girlish members of the student body and willing women faculty members. Josephine, as all the while predicted, rose to eminence as a major and often-quoted critic whose brilliance and fair-mindedness were of legendary dimensions: she was reputed to be Coleridge's equal, and Hazlitt's superior, in their chosen fields of letters. Honorary degrees were conferred on her by the vying universities, with Bob's being no exception. Bob closed his jealousy in secrecy, and plotted a more gruesome revenge than his clandestine adulteries. Josephine would have to be dishonored; to this profound end, Bob brought all his powers together, to evilly conspire. Josephine's downfall, her sordid disgrace, were being schemed. Bob was a laughingstock, for being the plodding consort of the reigning queen of the intellect. This was not to be borne lightly; he gathered his dark malice, and invoked devil-borrowed powers, to inspire a superb revenge to end Josephine as a threat. He must weaken her brain, to damage it beyond repair. That would enfeeble her faculties, she'd stop writing, her career would stop; her addiction to books would be forever paused. Till then, Bob couldn't rest. To resort to so foul a thing, to fell and arrest the too-endowed Josephine! To put a woman . . . in her place. This was to earn all men's gratitude, who had to endure superior loved ones. Thus Bob felt justified for his fallen deed.

VII

"It's righteous of me," he monologued one night. Josephine was in her study, finishing a critical masterpiece comparing all periods of literature with each other in terms of the prevailing conditions historical to their given societies; and she showed how civilized culture is molded by works of art, as well as reflected. This would revolutionize the study of history, literature, all of art, civilization, society, and culture. What an ambitious book to be written! It was her fame's prancing pinnacle, and on such an opus her already solid reputation would be so firmly established, so imperishably entrenched, that her universal significance would last forever as America's premier contribution to man as a reading animal. So too, monumentalized, would bristle the abstract of all masculine jealousy on Bob's suffering head. Thus darkened this husband's brooding to find a form of adversity of firmest ruin to so intellectual a wife and enemy. A fiend's agony wouldn't be enough. Perfection would have to breed a total harm to unsoar in full flight a woman paragon's exaltation of language and concept. Was it too big for destruction to undermine? Then boost destruction into a bigger might for this titanic accomplishment. The honor of all men, in every age, was the stake Bob would fight for, in bringing down this mere woman who simply did not know her place. Men have domination over the mind: Bob would enforce this.

Unaware of such unhusbandly intentions, Josephine was alternately writing and typing, to complete her crowning work. Her publisher was greedy for the manuscript. He had halted all other printing schedules, to prepare for this unprecedented priority. He would be arriving next morning in a taxi, with a metal suitcase with a lock, to take her typewritten pages in the sanctity of foolproof safekeeping. And he would have two armed escorts with him; the police had granted him this civil license, in this solemn wedding of an immense business breakthrough (of boon to the whole publishing enterprise on a huge economic scale) with a cultural event whose implications were of greater stupendor than the moon's American rape.

Well, Bob wasn't going to sit back and let it happen. He'd put an end to the myth of the passive male in America. His act would be of interference. To sabotage a woman's greatness would be the elevation of his whole gender, in this pronounced case. Bob and Josephine were symbols: the game at stake was the whole sexual race. To reaffirm man's primacy, was Bob's greater role.

To strike a woman off her high saddle, and land her back in her lowly functions of housekeeper, cook, and birthgiver, and sexual object and childtender. To strike for all reactionary grass roots, and return mankind to basics. To kill off the "women's liberation" campaign, so popular among radicals today.

Bob was a martyr in a cause of such sweep. He must pluck the head out of Josephine—if necessary by burning her manuscript to enrage her into madness and provoke her to a crime that all women would be punished for. To earn history's approbation for men, and her eternal condemnation of women, who would be struck from glory on the strength of Josephine's flop, her archangel-like fall from a false and literary grace. To restore some semblance of sanity, with men at rule.

VIII

Bob was determined to die, but Josephine would have to kill him. She'd value her manuscript, so he'd burn it. In her fury . . . Well, Bob would pay. But so would Josephine.

In the end, man would rise to regain his lead, in his eternal tussle with women for supremacy. Bob would historically redeem the balance, by making a villain of Josephine, with himself in the martyr role. But to be a martyr, he must make it seem that *he* did *not* burn the manuscript. He would have to plant the guilt on Josephine's head, while himself incurring her homicidal wrath. A difficult prize: necessity would have to battle for it. By one stroke of self-sacrificial cunning, Bob would overcome the cultivated lifetime of Josephine's flowering genius. That would even up those odds that mocked him so, in his outranked subjugation to a wife's eloquent erudition. The lowly must resort to tricks across the unflattering talent gap. Democracy upheld with poster idealism the brute jungle tactics that would blunt the refined and coarsen all edges. Equality advertised its justification, on any ground.

By luck, the telephone rang; a literary colleague of Josephine was calling, so she left her study to where the phone was waiting two rooms away. Bob prayed that the phone talk would be long-winded. Such a prospect would arm his opportunity with its crucially strengthened time. He crept into her study. But this was a modern apartment, and there was no fireplace. So he'd heat the oven and roast her pages there. He gathered up her extensive manuscript, minus an overflowing page or two, and cradled the bulging pack in both arms under his tickled chin. But she always made carbon copies! Laden with his burden, he searched for the carbon-copy manuscript. There it was, on an adjoining desk. What a time to get caught red-handed! He heaped the copy-manuscript onto the original, and staggered with an awkward load, to whose bulky mastery he felt frantically weakened, in a critical time. He wasn't cut out for crime. And he was caught. His wife returned. The phone call had been brief.

"An instinct of survival made me cut short that important call. I had a premonition that your jealously was up to something desperate, and would employ any ruse, even this very legitimate and unstaged phone summons, to expedite your dirty work afoot. Here's a hysterical proposition for you. I caught you flat-footed, and look how foolish you are, trembling red-veined under a wife's envied product. I have one recourse: to divorce you."

Bob relieved himself by replacing the manuscript on the desks, both copies back in their proper place, like an abashed but dutiful son obediently atoning for surreptitious offense which the parent condescended to notice. "You have the upper hand, I think," was Bob's rejoinder. Josephine would have to dispatch the case quickly, mercifully or not, according to an expedient verdict that would get her back to her desk to add the finishing touches to a work of far greater weight than her simpleton husband. The publisher would taxi-arrive by the morning, with his expensive precautions of ceremonious practicality. It must be ready by then for him. First, to get rid of Bob, and disarm him morally, to reduce his will against another attempt of final treachery to a spouse. He was so easy to detect, but it was time-consuming, and emotionally taxing. How could she placate his envy? The man needed reassuring. His male vanity—could she restore it? How could she seem weak? She must beguile him into an illusion of his power. She must appeal to his pity, by deceptively arousing his protective might. But this was impossible. She, a published author, he, a puny professor! The obvious odds were stacked in her impressive favor.

IX

"No more mischief, please. If I catch you at such another bungled undermining of me, my work, my career, I'm going to have you locked up, for I'm friends with the police chief, who's a literary buff in his spare time. I know what you're up to. Can you cut it out? If not, a jail sentence will ruin your university tenure prospects, and eliminate all your academic ambitions to one day rise to dean or to the departmental chair. How would you like that, dear?"

"I stand chastised, and if you'll only cease intimidating me—which is so very easy for you to do—I vow never to obstruct your greatness or impede the strides of your genius in the triumphs of bearing publishing fruit. I'll take a back seat, to your foremost rank in our marital inequality. But may I suggest . . . a pride-restoring compromise?"

"I'm busy, so be brief. What is it?"

"Let's produce a child. Let's take off our contraceptive devices, which we've been careful to keep on till now, to allow your industrious enterprise and prolific literary purpose to prosper. Can't you extend your fertility to motherhood as well? For then our child would have your brilliance, but my vanity. And I could identify with your superiority through the vehicle of our *common meeting ground:* the child we will both share. In our joint ownership, I'll be reconciled to my lesser importance. Our essences will be merged, in the same child, as a symbolic union. Then I'll recognize your greatness, accord you its privilege, with no bitter envy. I'll love you as you are: and encourage you to work even harder as the critical lioness of our day, to accumulate a truly prodigal authorship. Our bloodsteams will be mingled in our baby, your genius with my mediocrity. I'll then be a part of you, through the kid. That will redeem my faith in myself, and make my manhood less shaky when linked with your mental dominance through the biological equalizer that levels power out evenly and allots the greater share to the lesser, in a balance appeasing to my vanity, rendering my homocidal hostility against you harmless and redundant by eliminating a bitter cause in an overall blend of love and family. Our differences won't matter, then. It'll work very well for me. Your output will be acceptable, and not a challenge. By vanquishing the threat, I'll be your toothless spouse, paternally your equal, by love's family institution. And it will save our marriage. Can you match this plan with your consent, on an equal footing of wills? I offer you unvying love, and will bar competition as a plane of masculine strife. That will ease life for you, and your leisure will go on, unabated—but consolidated maritally, having been given my conjugal blessing—to create ever excellent works of criticism. It's good for you, it's good for me, this plan. What do you say?"

"It would work, except that I've stopped loving you. My work is foremost, and you've receded dreadfully, till my life can find no consequence in you. I resolve to rid myself of you and call it quits. Until then, my freedom couldn't be called my own. Be understanding and see my point of view. You won't stand in my way, once you find it my better welfare to be devoid of your company. I yearn for the old solitude, minus you. Now I want to return to work. The morning will soon bring my publisher. That's so much more urgent than you. You always come last in the priority stakes. This drains your vanity away, with the rage to compensate emboldened to criminal fury. You're well rid of me. I'll abjure you. Shut the door, behind you. Tomorrow we'll part. It's the only way, in all full dignity. Your pride is low when you live with me. Released to freedom, you'll gain your steady level, and pursue your best life, without competitive interference. Accept our oncoming divorce. It must be, perforce."

X

She was locked in her room, working. Bob was outcast. His exile had been announced, and the matter closed shut. He had an abandoned soul to nurse: his own, alas.

Bob was staggered, and wept. Her declaration of rejection carved a brutal finish on his total humiliation and polished the abuse of his ego to an extent he could never recover from. Josephine had administered the *coup de grâce*, by ruthlessly turning down his domestic rescue suggestion that would patch up their differences. The hour was eerily late. He had a morbid night.

He could but submit. To ponder anything else would be futile. Her will had been made clear. He was too passive now for hate and murder. He had been drained of violence. Numbness and repose were the peaceful remedies, for fury had shown itself impotent. He would humbly absorb this defeat. The trial was at an end. How could Josephine be opposed? He would worship that majestic queen. From afar. His role would be: her former husband. It would calm his dignity and weigh his solace over with tragedy's dramatic balm. To be the toppled consort, to live out his days in philosophy's pale glamor over a meditative soul. To sink away, serenely. To leave Josephine alone, but claim her in enshrined memory, the inaccessible he had once laid claim to, before mystic renunciation took his pride away, eased his manhood out, and left him in romantic reverie. Ah, what a sweet thing. To be lessened into glory. And to will the soul away.

He was asleep at dawn. Josephine had finished her work. She found him, sleeping benignly, sitting slouched on an armchair. She knew she had won. She was hers, alone. But by work, it was to the world she belonged. Fame had commended her. Soon the doorbell would ring. Her devout publisher would appear. He would ease her of her product. And she would gain renown. Renown was hers already. She served literature. She had more to give.

SINCE MARY

WALTER S. HAMADY

FOR MARY,

the invisible blood
travelling thru the eyes
making the color gain
in spots that see and
take all the world into the head

next to last plumfoot pœm

constellations have shown
and shrunk through the
successive seasons and
go on passing men
fooling with the moon

and we are no closer to
anything but what we are

in the first place

you would limit the seasons to
summer, lay in the sun like dried fruit
and smoke successive cigarettes.

I would not.

your
last letter came with mobilgas
whose punched holes had more random purpose
than yours

the last plumfoot pœm

your lips may
pout wrong now
and your breasts
not perk
the same.

I think let's
not have this
further inspection
let's let it slide on past
and stay water
cress growing
in this spring going
year round.

slow thaw

the spring rain
has fallen
intermittently
for two whole days and

mostly went into the ground
except for puddles
where it couldn't anymore.

I'm sure
you've met
people like that

ten on one/1

days have fled
since I've spoken
to myself of

concerns disregarding
themselves of all else
that might be
of interest.

but the weather
has spoken in
fifteen days straight
of rain   :
a statement of influence.

ten on one/5

reasons shed
their need of time
in silence.

what things leave us
are not needed
and become
separate

again, alone
in the atavism of time
as much un influenced
as many days of
oppressive weather.

ten on one/9

how few days
actually pass
slowly

and at once
how much gets done
as singular acts,
couple to make love,

occur simply as folds
in an open curtain
standing to each side
of a rainy day
that seems endless.

friends

my friends have
let me live
giving me over to know
my joy as theirs
without the panagraphic manipulation
what   so   ever

just plain exchange
of daily takeplacenesses, sometimes
nothing more

never expectations

as for the rest of it
Consumers Union
might give a better report
on washing machines

living

some people
are regular & reasonable & steady

some are long about it & long
at doing things and

others are : long at it but
get nothing   or
save it up and let it go all
at once while
others are irregular
with no pattern to,
or consciousness of

it

mom said, people live a lot
just like the way they shit. *

for barto's father

good ideas
come all the time
especially
in the shower

but they get forgot

if towels
would be notebooks
the wasted time
could be form in them

the pile of moments
could be blotted up

but parts of life
must pass empty—
the alternating current
so to speak

for mark potvin

hunting wild asparagus
in my mind
along the fence by the lack of time
I've always spent
not knowing what to call things.

things are things.
you never use a word
when you can point and be
with whatever it is things are.

farm lights

in the evening,
the stars
come down to fill
the dark fields
in the forms of fireflies
and have conversations
about the miles of milkweeds
standing along the road.

then the morning stars
linger and get confused
with the farmer's dusk to
dawn lights
which keep yellow-greenish
the night that even he,
a man of the land, can't stand
to leave dark.

kennelly/heavyside layer

some nights
in this valley
local stations fade and blurr
so that it's hard to get anything
except Nashville or St Louis
eight hundred miles away.

according to the grass is greener
principle, it happens to people too,
and after the rhythm & the blues
the news doesn't make as much sense .

going on daylight saving time

night comes
one hour later
all across the united states

but the birds are heedless
and sing crepuscular songs
one hour earlier as
is their program.
spring and summer merge
and before you know it
it's fall, it's one hour earlier,
all the birds leave

and leave you
with nothing to say except
welcome winter.

as autumn begins

as autumn begins,
from this farmhouse window
where I live,
and for some time prior
the small white clusters of
Heath Asters
cover the hills and valleys.

it is this september snow
that brings out a certain small butterfly
in profusion equal to the flowers.

close to the ground
and at all heights of the air
these little butterflies
flutter like the leaves
and disturb the balance of my eye.

page fifteen

this old farmhouse
is alive with the noise of
dying flies
trying to escape the cold.

the leaves hurry by
in lowering sunlight
and are quick as wind
across the grass through the fence.

there's not much lingering
or slow this time of year

except our woodpile
standing large and neat
against the house and
winter on its way down
from up north of here.

oak stuff

dear mary,
please be nice to me.
go on saying .
that you think I'm a nice man
even when not.

call me to the window
in the evening to see a western.
never permit me a tv set.

keep on being cheerful
and get your rest—
if I am slow to come then
think of the oaks at this latitude
are the last to bear their leaves,

yet make the strongest
of all structures .

I never tell my wife I love her

gregory peck walked into a new york restaurant
and asked for
a table (
             did you hear this one   ?   )

the head waiter,   not
recognizing him said he'd see what he could do,
the place being busy with people,   &
got lost in them.

meantime,

gregory peck's friend
who was along said : tell him who you are
                        tell him
                        who you are
and
gregory peck said: if
you gotta tellem who
you are   you   ain't .

THREE POEMS

DENISE LEVERTOV

GANDHI'S GUN (AND BRECHT'S VOW)

Vessels of several
shapes and sizes—

bowls, pots,
a tall vase

and the guitar's
waiting body:

forms drawn
by a hand's
energy.
   'Never

  run away from the stormcenter.

   Cultivate

  cool courage, die without killing'—

Strong orange, deep
oil-pastel green

but at the center, strange
upstroke of black

stronger, deeper
than all,

—'but if one has not

that courage'—

(or singing *'Keiner
oder Alle. Alles
oder Nichts!'*)

—'cultivate

the art of killing and being killed

rather than in a cowardly manner

to flee from danger.'

Vessels, counterparts
of the human; primal
vessel of music

towards which like a rifle
that harsh stroke blackly
points upward

would fail, fall from their whirling
dance, without

the terror patiently
poised there,

ultimate focus.

CASA FELICE   I

for Jim and Reed

Getting back into
ordinary gentle morning, tide
    wavelessly dreaming in,
    silent gulls at ease on wheatsheaf sandbars—

Off the limb of
desperation
      I drop
      plumb into peace for a day—

it's
  not easy.
      But easier—
          O blessed
          blue!
     —than fear and reason
     supposed of late.

CASA FELICE   II

for Richard

Richard, if you were here
would you too be peaceful?

(I am angry
all of the time, not just sometimes,
you said. We must
smash the state.
Smash the state.)

If you were here
for these two days at Casa
Felice, if you were here and listened
to the almost soundless tide
incoming,
            what would it say to you?
Would you feel new
coldness towards me
because this April morning, gentle light
on the unglittering sea and pale sands,
I am not angry and not tense?

NOTES ON CONTRIBUTORS

WALTER ABISH was born in Vienna, spent part of his childhood in China, and lived for a number of years in Israel before coming to the United States. He has contributed fiction to *Confrontation* and poetry to the *New American Review*. *Duel Site*, a book of his poems, was recently brought out by Tibor de Nagy Editions, and he is now completing a novel: *The Galactic Dictionary or V.V.*

ROBERT BLY, whose *The Light Around the Body* won him the National Book Award for poetry in 1968, donated his prize money to the Resistance. His most recent books include a translation from the Norwegian of Knut Hamsun's *Hunger* (Farrar, Straus & Giroux), a collection of prose poems called *The Morning Glory* (Kayak Press) and an anthology, *Forty Poems Touching on Recent American History*. He lives in Madison, Minnesota.

BESMILR BRIGHAM was a 1970 recipient of a fellowship grant from the National Endowment for the Arts. She was born in Mississippi, and now lives in Arkansas, but has spent much time among the Indians of Mexico and Central America, which has deeply influenced her work. Her most recent books are *Heaved from the Earth* (Alfred A. Knopf), *The Rain Bush Field (Poems from Mexico)* (ARX Foundation/Summit Press), *Open Structures: Poems of Saints and Grace* (The Crossing Press) and *Agony Dance: Death of the Dancing Dolls* (Prensa de Lagar/Wine Press).

Two recent collections of poems by WILLIAM BRONK have been published by James Weil at the Elizabeth Press (103 Van Etten Boulevard, New Rochelle, N.Y.). Bronk's earlier work, *The World, the Worldless*, was brought out jointly in 1964 by New Directions and San Francisco Review, and his "Copan Essays" appeared in *Origin 10*. He lives in Hudson Falls, New York.

For ÁLVARO DE CAMPOS, see the contributor's note on FERNANDO PESSOA and the translator's note preceding "Maritime Ode."

MARVIN COHEN was born in Brooklyn and lived for many years on Manhattan's Lower East Side. Three of his stories have appeared in previous ND annuals (nos. 18, 19 and 21), and New Directions published his first long work of fiction, *The Self-Devoted Friend,* in 1968. He now teaches English composition at the City College of the City University of New York.

Born in 1919 in Oakland, California, ROBERT DUNCAN lived in New York during the Second World War, where he edited *Experimental Review,* and returned to the West Coast to study medieval and Renaissance history from 1947 to 1950. He contributed in the early 1950's to such periodicals as *Origin* and *The Black Mountain Review* and was active in the emergent San Francisco literary scene. A prolific poet, a selected list of his published books includes *Roots and Branches* (1964) and *Bending the Bow* (1968), both brought out by New Directions, *The Opening of the Field* (Grove), *The Years As Catches, Poems 1939–1946* (Oyez), *Medea at Colchis* (Oyez), *The Cat and the Blackbird* (White Rabbit Press) and *Heavenly City, Earthly City* (Porter). Duncan now lives in San Francisco, and among his current projects is a long book on the Imagist poet H.D. (Hilda Doolittle), the first volume of which will be published this year by Black Sparrow Press.

New Directions published *The Very Thing That Happens,* RUSSELL EDSON's book of fables illustrated with his own drawings, in 1964, and an excerpt from his unpublished novel, *The Horsecock Chair,* appeared in *ND 20.* Edson printed two earlier books of fables and drawings himself at Thing Press (149 Weed Avenue, Stamford, Conn.), *Appearances* and *A Stone is Nobody's,* and in 1969 Jonathan Williams published *What a Man Can See* in his Jargon Series, with drawings by Ray Johnson.

The range and energy of LAWRENCE FERLINGHETTI's activities in the current social-cultural revolution are impressive. He is involved in protest movements, reads on TV, for recordings, and at colleges around the country, keeps an eye on his City Lights bookstore in San Francisco, brings out many important *avant-garde* literary texts in his City Lights paperbooks, has his plays produced in college and off-Broadway theaters . . . and has published four new books at New Directions within a span of two years: *The Secret*

Meaning of Things (poems); the political tirade *Tyrannus Nix?*, which has a wide "extra" circulation in Vietnam among GI's who mimeograph it for hand-to-hand distribution; *The Mexican Night*, the first installment of his ongoing travel journals; and, most recently, *Back Roads to Far Places*, a sequence of brief, haikulike lyrics and meditations, inspired by Bashō and Milarepa, produced with his own calligraphy and drawings.

CHARLES HENRI FORD's association with ND is long standing. A contributor to several earlier annuals, both as author and guest editor of special sections, his translations of Baudelaire *(The Mirror of Baudelaire)* were brought out in the Poets of the Year Series in 1942, and a volume of his own poetry, *Sleep in a Nest of Flames*, in 1949. Later collections include his *Selected Poems* (Black Sparrow Press), *Spare Parts* (Horizon) and an anthology, *The Avant Gard in "View"* (Horizon). Ford spends part of each year in Greece and recently has been making a film.

DAVID GIANNINI was born in 1948 and lives in New York City. His work has appeared in *Sanskaras*, and he has received the Osa and Lee Mays award for poetry. He co-edits, with Richard Meyers, a small literary magazine.

WALTER S. HAMADY, who was born in 1940, now lives in Mt. Horeb, Wisconsin, where he and his wife, Mary, publish handprinted, limited editions of contemporary poetry at The Perishable Press. His "Plum-foot Poems" appeared in *New Direction 21*.

YUKI HARTMAN was born in Japan and now lives in New York City. Genesis:Grasp Press has brought out a pamphlet of twenty-seven of his poems, *a One of me*.

LAWSON FUSAO INADA is on the faculty of Southern Oregon College. His first book of poetry, *Before the War*, is scheduled to be published this year by William Morrow.

DENISE LEVERTOV and her husband, the novelist Mitchell Goodman, are active leaders in the movement to stop the war in Indochina. Her two most recent books, published by New Directions, are *Relearning the Alphabet* (1970) and a translation from the French of the *Selected Poems* of Guillevic. She is teaching this year at Kirkland College in Clinton, New York.

Biographical information on ENRIQUE LIHN will be found in the translators' note preceding his "Two Poems." WILLIAM WITHERUP teaches creative writing at Soledad Correctional Facility in Soledad, California. His work is included in *Quickly Aging Here: Some Poet's of the 1970's* (Anchor), and Lillabulero Press has brought out *The Sangre de Cristo Mountain Poems.* SERGE ECHEVERRIA is a native Chilean who now makes his home in San Francisco. With Witherup, he translated three poems by Nicanor Parra that appeared in the *Tri-Quarterly* Latin American anthology, as well as a selection of twenty-five poems by Lihn, *The Endless Malice* (Lillabulero Press: Krums Corners, R.D. 3, Ithaca, N.Y.).

Born and raised in Kentucky, the young poet RICHARD MEYERS now lives in New York, where he is co-editor, with David Giannini, of *Genesis: Grasp.* Some of his work appeared in *New Directions 22.*

Biographical information on FERNANDO PESSOA (ÁLVARO DE CAMPOS) will be found in the translator's note preceding "Maritime Ode." EDWIN HONIG is a member of the Department of English at Brown University. His translation of Pessoa's *Selected Poems,* the first collection of the poet's Portuguese work to appear in English, is to be brought out by the Swallow Press, with an extensive introduction by Octavio Paz. Included among Honig's other works are *García Lorca,* a critical guide (New Directions), *Dark Conceit: The Making of Allegory* and *Spring Journal: Poems* (Wesleyan).

JAMES PURDY lives in Brooklyn Heights. His story "On the Rebound," together with some poems, was first brought out in a limited edition by John Martin at the Black Sparrow Press. New Directions publishes two Purdy collections, *Children Is All* (stories and two short plays) and *Color of Darkness* (stories), and recordings of the author reading from his own works have been released by Spoken Arts. His most recent novel is *Jeremy's Vision* (Doubleday), the first in a trilogy about Middle Western towns to be called *Sleepers in Moon-Crowned Valleys.*

CARL RAKOSI's early work appeared in such seminal anthologies and magazines as Ezra Pound's *The Exile, The Objectivists Anthology* and *The Little Review*. New Directions published his *Selected Poems* in 1941, as well as his most recent collection, *Amulet*, in 1967. He received an award from the National Endowment for the arts in 1969, and that same year his five tape recordings for introductory courses in literature, entitled *Possibilities in Poetry*, were brought out by Amidon Associates, and an "Interview with Carl Rakosi" appeared in the spring number of *Contemporary Literature*. He spent 1969–70 as writer-in-residence at the University of Wisconsin (Madison).

Biographical information on YANNIS RITSOS will be found in the translator's note preceding "The Moonlight Sonata." RAE DALVEN is chairman of the English Department at Ladycliff College, Highland Falls, New York. Her anthology of *Modern Greek Poetry* (Gaer Associates) was brought out in 1950, and her translation of *The Complete Poems of Cafavy* (Harcourt, Brace & World) in 1961.

DENNIS SILK, who has been living in Jerusalem since 1955, is now on active reserve duty in the Israeli army. "Porfiri and Esthalina" is part of a work in miscellaneous forms about Jerusalem, a sequence that includes stories, poems, puppet-plays and brief fables. Another section, "Montefiore," appeared in *New Directions 22*, and "Tryphon," the first of the series, was published in *Encounter*.

GARY SNYDER's latest collection of poetry, *Regarding Wave*, was published last year by New Directions. Born in San Francisco in 1930, he grew up in the Pacific Northwest, was graduated in 1951 from Reed College in anthropology and literature, and from 1953 to 1956 was engaged in Japanese and Chinese studies at Berkeley and worked in the woods and at sea. From 1956 to 1968 he lived mostly in Japan, and traveled through India. A Bollingen Foundation grant recipient and Guggenheim Fellow, his books include *Riprap* (1959), *Myths and Texts* (1960), *Riprap and Cold Mountain Poems* (1965), *Six Sections from Mountains and Rivers without End* (1965), *The Back Country* (1968) and *Earth House Hold* (1969). Ecology is now one of Snyder's major concerns, and he is a leader in the movement to save our natural environment. Last summer he built a house for his family in the foothills of the Sierras in California.

Don Wulffson, who teaches English and remedial reading at San Fernando High School in Los Angeles, is the author of two textbooks for the educationally handicapped. He was born in 1943 and has spent most of his life in California.